WORKPLACE BULLYING

It's Just Bad for Business

Prevention, Management, &
Elimination Strategies for
Organizations & Everyone Else

Paul Pelletier, LL.B. PMP

ISBN print: 978-0-9950036-0-6
ISBN ebook: 978-0-9950036-1-3

Disclaimer

It is important to note that the advice and examples in this book are intended as a guide only. The contents of this book do not constitute legal advice and aren't a substitute for specific legal advice or opinions. It may be appropriate to seek the help of professionals (legal, health care, and others) depending on the nature of the situation.

All the stories in this book are real. Further, the examples may resemble other people's bullying situations because many bullies exhibit similar behaviors. Such resemblance is purely coincidental. Names used have been changed and have no reference to real persons. Organizations are not revealed in respect of their privacy.

Finally, the opinions within this book are those of the author's alone and don't represent the opinions of any organization or the publisher.

The information provided herein is stated to be truthful and consistent, in that any liability, in terms of inattention or otherwise, by use or abuse of any policies, processes, or directions contained within is the solitary and utter responsibility of the recipient reader. Under no circumstance will any legal responsibility or blame be held against the publisher or author for any reparation, damages, or monetary loss due to the information herein, either directly or indirectly.

All rights reserved

Published by
Diversity Publishing
Vancouver, Canada

Acknowledgments

The beginning is the most important part of the work.

— Plato

I want to thank all the courageous people who have shared their stories about workplace bullying. As a frequent presenter at conferences and workshops throughout the world, I'm constantly reminded that the bullying experience I thought I was enduring in silence is actually one that thousands of others relate to. You are the inspiration for this book. It is my sincere hope that, together, we will become better informed and empowered to take action to raise awareness and create a zero tolerance for bullying in our workplaces.

To those who supported me in this unexpected personal and professional journey, I owe much gratitude. From a traditional career in the legal and business world to an advocate against workplace bullying – thank you for encouraging me to remain focused in the pursuit of a higher purpose.

To my friends and family who suffered while I was in the midst of the bullying hurricane and supported me through the fallout and re-building process – thank you for your patience, compassion, and guidance.

To the medical professionals who cared for me and helped me heal both physically and mentally – you gave me back my health and passion to take the bully and organization supporting him to task. Despite the odds and result, I firmly believe that we have a choice to be powerless or face our fears head-on. With that higher purpose, I find inspiration from others much wiser than I.

Table of Contents

Introduction

Everyone ... likely has a bullying story, whether as the victim, bully, or as a witness.
— Michael M. Honda[1]

Fifteen years ago, the word "bullying" was a word used almost exclusively in the context of our schools and the suffering of children at the hands of cruel classmates. The world has woken up to the reality of this behavior in broader contexts. We now hear about bullying almost every day, still in our schools and on the Internet, but with rapidly growing regularity in our workplaces.

Bullying in the workplace is a significant global problem that, just like cancer or economics, ignores the borders of culture, nationality, gender, class, age, or other traditional distinction. It not only causes harm to those in the target zone of the bullies but also has enormous negative impacts to the workplace culture, projects, programs, profits, and success of our organizations.

I challenge you to Google "workplace bullying" as a starting point. There are many useful articles, research papers, stories, and websites dedicated to the topic and even a Workplace Bullying Institute. The United Kingdom has a National Workplace Bullying Advice Line. As one U.S. TV newscast described it, the "dirty little workplace secret" of workplace bullying is being fully exposed.

It may also come as a surprise to know that there are

many YouTube videos about workplace bullying – everything from TED Talks[2] to TV news and journalistic essays on the topic. In short, there is an abundance of useful and readily available information, research, and tools for preventing, identifying, and addressing workplace bullying.

Yet, despite a wealth of data and reasons why organizations should take action to eliminate bullying, they rarely do. Further, the actions they often take prove ineffective because they don't understand bullying. With organizations failing to stop bullying, governments are taking on the issue.

Many countries have acknowledged that workplace bullying poses a risk to workers and most of the Western world has enacted anti-bullying legislation to protect workers. These laws have led the charge to force organizations to implement training and programs to address workplace bullying.

I'm neither a counselor nor a psychologist. While I consulted with respected workplace bullying experts from those fields, I didn't collaborate with any of them to write this book. Thus, my approach to defining and addressing bullying is through the lens of the average business person, manager, or employee. It is also through the lens of a person who has experienced bullying and through the experiences of others. By no means am I ignoring that there are often deeper and complex psychological factors at play in the dynamic of workplace bullying. I leave that analysis for other experts whose talent and advice has helped many organizations. Throughout the book, I also recommend when the use of counseling, psychology, and conflict resolution experts is advisable. However, my focus is on a straightforward, simplified approach designed to motivate the business world to take action to address bullying.

This book is dedicated to enhancing awareness of workplace bullying and the range of diabolical impacts it creates for people and organizations. I also hope to empower those who face bullying directly – the victims (commonly called a "target" in the context of workplace bullying), coworkers, managers, and executives. Most of us lack the skills or information to objectively identify and appreciate the motivation behind workplace bullying. By providing useful and non-judgmental information, tips, and tools you will be better able to cope and to take action.

The good news is that increased public awareness, recent research, and expanding illegalization of workplace bullying have paved the way for efforts to prevent it and eliminate it. Both employees and their employers are becoming more acutely aware of the impacts and costs associated with bullying. Bullying thrives in silence, with targets and coworkers feeling too intimidated to confront the bully or complain. If managers, human resources personnel, and senior level executives take initiative in addressing bullying early on, much larger financial, ethical, legal, stakeholder, and project problems will be avoided. Eventually, it is my hope that these initiatives will lead to wider support for zero tolerance for bullying in the workplace regardless of circumstance, societal norm, or jurisdiction.

1

The Anatomy of Bullying

The time is always right to do what is right.
— Martin Luther King[1]

Bullying can be as harmful in the workplace as it is in schools and other areas of society, causing the well-understood emotional and physical impacts, plus a long list of challenges for employees and their organizations. More sobering are the clear and irrefutable statistics – workplace bullying is costing businesses billions of dollars annually. For every short-term result that a bully achieves, there is a list of longer-term negative business impacts that far outweigh any temporary benefits. To quote Patricia Barnes, a workplace bullying author, judge, and attorney, workplace bullying is likely the "single most preventable and needless expense on a company's register."[2]

A conversation about bullying should start with recognition of the ethical and leadership dilemma it creates. Hopefully, we all agree that supporting, condoning, or fostering bullying is unethical and not "what is right." Ethical behavior is part of an essential foundation for trust that we all must earn in order to succeed.

This is not only my opinion, but has been underscored by some of the most important thought leaders of our time.

The Leadership Challenge by Kouzes and Posner is the gold standard for research-based leadership and is a premier resource for aspiring leaders. The text informs us that leadership requires trust:

> *It's clear that if people anywhere are to willingly follow someone – whether it be into battle or into the boardroom, the front office or the front lines – they first want to assure themselves that the person is worthy of their trust.*[3]

All our work is, for the most part, an activity undertaken in concert with others. While we may refer to these others as team members, stakeholders, or coworkers, we depend on them for the success of our organizations. If employees don't trust or feel supported by their leaders, there will be no motivation or commitment to fully engage.

Following this logic, without effective ethical leadership (which includes responding to bullying) there will be few fully engaged and high-performance teams, and even fewer program, project, and innovation successes. Think of the organizational impacts that flow from this result – all at the hands of a workplace bully.

From this place of appreciation that bullying is unethical and creating preventable impacts on our organizations, we can begin to study the behaviors of bullies. We can also create strategies for identifying and addressing bullying in our workplaces.

What Is Workplace Bullying?

As strange as it seems, one of the most-asked questions I get is: "What exactly is workplace bullying?" This is entirely understandable because, as of the date of publication of this book, there is still no definition for "workplace bullying" in *Merriam Webster's Dictionary*.[4]

> Knowledge is power. Information is liberating. Education is the premise of progress, in every society, in every family.
>
> *Kofi Annan, Former Secretary-General of the United Nations[5]*

This seems unfathomable considering "pleather," "sexting," "LOL," and other contemporary words can be found.

After I gave a recent presentation on workplace bullying, a woman I'll call Janice approached me in tears. She always wondered what was going on with her boss, but she simply couldn't place her finger on a proper identifier for the daily attacks she was facing. It wasn't until she saw a definition of "workplace bullying" that it became clear. The more examples of bullying behavior she had heard, the more emotional she had become. She told me the presentation lifted a massive weight off her – simply because she now had the right label to call her bullying boss.

Given the lack of dictionary definition, we must rely on other sources to define bullying. Fortunately, there are a number of highly respected and internationally renowned psychologists, professors, authors, and researchers on workplace bullying, including Professor Ståle Einarsen (University of Bergen, Norway), Clare Rayner, Lyn Quine (University of Canterbury, UK), and Professor Sir Carey Lyne Cooper (University of Manchester, UK) to name a few. According to Einarsen, bullying at work means:

> ... *harassing, offending, socially excluding someone or negatively affecting someone's work tasks. In order for the label bullying (or mobbing) to be applied to a particular activity, interaction, or process it has to occur repeatedly and regularly (e.g. weekly) and over a period of time (e.g. about*

six months). Bullying is an escalated process in the course of which the person confronted ends up in an inferior position and becomes the target of systematic negative social acts.[6]

For those who appreciate a more concise definition, the Workplace Bullying Institute defines workplace bullying as:

Repeated, health-harming mistreatment, verbal abuse, or conduct which is threatening, humiliating, intimidating, or sabotage that interferes with work, or some combination of the three.[7]

It is important to distinguish from bullying the inappropriate, one-time acts of someone who is under a great deal of pressure, having a particularly (and unusually) bad day, or handling a disagreement poorly. These are single events from which the perpetrator quickly and sincerely apologizes. They understand they've offended and are accountable. A bully's actions, on the other hand, are repetitive, intentional, and deviant. They deflect accountability and can't be reasoned with.

As previously noted, in many Western countries bullying is recognized as a form of workplace violence and a hazard to workers' health. For example, the United States Department of Labor, National Institute of Occupation Safety and Health Administration's definition of "Workplace Violence" incorporates many of the foundational characteristics of bullying, including:

Any act or threat of physical violence, harassment, intimidation, or other threatening disruptive behavior that occurs at the work site.[8]

One of the difficult aspects of bullying that many find hard to grasp is that it has nothing to do with work itself. It is driven by the bully's personal agenda, based on a warped perception of who they find threatening. To complicate matters, workplace bullies are sometimes hard to identify clearly. They can be highly skilled yet socially manipulative, targeting "weaker" employees while adept at charming those they think will serve their career path well. Bullies are usually focused on achieving results, regardless of means, ethics, or fairness. Sadly, it is often those results that senior managers are impressed with and focus on.

Overlooking the staff turnover, absences, team dysfunction, and low employee engagement levels, there are many stories where the bully's senior manager or supervisor says, "John seems great to me." Often, the higher-ups are well aware that John really is a bully, but instead describe him as "difficult," "runs a tight ship," "hard to get along with," or that he "suffers no fools." They ignore what they know deep down is bullying, because the short-term results trump the other considerations.

Bullies also create a real-life *Devil Wears Prada*[9] situation where everyone except those who work for the bully both fear and revere her at the same time. For outsiders, she is a symbol of the pinnacle of achievement or an iconic visionary. However, they also know that she is a force best not confronted and that you never want to be on her bad side or "hit list." Those underneath her are ruled by intimidation, workplace terrorism, and appallingly unreasonable expectations. Driven by their insatiable egos, bullies see compassion, kindness, and fairness as weakness. The workplace is their battlefield and winner takes all.

***

Workplace bullying is mistreatment perpetrated by an employee severe enough to compromise a targeted worker's health, jeopardize her or his job and career, and strain relationships with friends and family. It is deliberate, repetitive, disrespectful behavior that is always for the bully's benefit. It is a focused, systematic campaign of interpersonal destruction. All bullying can be categorized as a form of abuse.

> I have no right, by anything I do or say, to demean a human being in his own eyes. What matters is not what I think of him; it is what he thinks of himself. To undermine a man's self-respect is a sin.
>
> *Antoine de Saint-Exupery[10]*

Typical Bullying Behaviors

Bullies play by a simple zero-sum game mentality – the bullies see that their targets have something the bullies don't, and they will do whatever they need to in order to secure that "something" or take it away. In the process, they may destroy the target as well. I have heard hundreds of stories about workplace bullying from every sector, profession, culture, and type of organization and corner of the world. There are threads of behavior that wind through most bullying stories. While each bully adopts their own form of workplace terrorism, bullying usually includes behaviors that can be categorized into three types, as outlined in the following pages (this is a list of representative examples and isn't exhaustive).

Aggressive Communication
- Eye rolling, intentionally interrupting, shutting down conversations
- Insulting or making offensive remarks
- Shouting, yelling, angry outbursts
- Going around coworkers in order to avoid communicating with them
- Harsh finger-pointing, invasion of personal space, shoving, blocking the way
- Staring others down, giving dirty looks
- Sending angry emails or other e-communication
- Humiliating or ridiculing, excessive teasing

- Spreading rumors or gossip
- Ignoring peers when they walk by
- Playing harsh practical jokes
- Taunting with the use of social media

Manipulation of Work

- Removing tasks imperative to job responsibilities
- Giving unmanageable workloads & impossible deadlines
- Arbitrarily changing tasks
- Using employee evaluations to document supposed poor work quality without setting goals or providing the tools needed to improve

Sabotaging Work

- Hinting that someone should quit, nobody likes him or her, or the boss thinks they are incompetent
- Withholding pertinent information needed to do one's job effectively
- Leaving employees out of communication loops
- Excessive micromanagement
- Failing to give credit, or stealing credit for others' work
- Preventing access to opportunities like promotions or raises
- Consistently pointing out mistakes, however little or long ago they occurred

***

Combining the requirements for repetition, deliberateness, and disrespectfulness with this list of behaviors usually results in the successful identification of a bully (or not). Bullying isn't a personality clash or a relationship conflict – it is abusive behavior that you can identify.

What Isn't Workplace Bullying?

Not every unpleasant or challenging conflict with people at work or on a project is bullying. On the contrary, conflict is a normal part of life and, as you may know too well, conflict in our pressure- and deadline-filled workplaces is often normal. So, it's important to contrast normal work behavior and interaction, particularly in uncomfortable and difficult times, from bullying.

For example, Sebastian shared his problems about a workplace relationship with a coworker. He works in the field of healthcare in a hospital surrounded by doctors, health crises, stressed-out families, sick patients, and focused healthcare workers. Everyone has his or her own agendas, concerns, and pressures. His work environment is stress-filled, ego-oriented, and decisions are made under pressure with life-and-death implications.

Sebastian described an ongoing battle with Kim, his coworker. As I heard him talking about their differences of opinion, opposing views on how to manage patients, and blow-ups in the emergency room, it was apparent to me that their conflict wasn't a bullying problem. It was a case of two professionals with strong and divergent opinions trying to achieve the same goal – improving patient results. They fought over small decisions. Kim wasn't picking on him every day. She wasn't humiliating him or sabotaging his work. The worst fights happened in stressful patient crises. This was a case of normal workplace conflict. Kim wasn't a bully. Kim and Sebastian needed to sit down, reason out their differences, and develop a respectful relationship.

> **For good ideas and true innovation, you need human interaction, conflict, argument, debate.**
>
> *Margaret Heffernan, Businesswoman*[11]

Here are some helpful examples of reasonable and regular conflicts that take place at work that wouldn't qualify as bullying, unless they also involved the behaviors noted in the definition of bullying:

Respectfully expressing differences of opinion.

Heated debates about divergent views on how to approach or resolve a challenge are normal. Sometimes they are even healthy and should be encouraged as they ensure that all opinions are considered. Challenging each other's opinions is standard behavior in competitive and high-performance team environments. Having to defend your position might be uncomfortable but it isn't inappropriate unless you are being humiliated and diminished in the process.

Offering constructive feedback, guidance, or advice about work-related behavior.

The key word here is "constructive." We all should have the emotional maturity to appreciate our flaws and areas for improvement. In a positive work environment, everyone is challenged to learn, grow, and develop. In order to do that, we need to be open and accepting of helpful and reasonable feedback delivered in a respectful way. Again, we may not like it or it may make us uncomfortable, but as long as the delivery mechanism is respectful, this isn't bullying.

Reasonable actions related to staff performance (i.e., managing performance, taking reasonable disciplinary actions, or assigning work).

Performance management will always be challenging. Communicating that expectations haven't been met isn't easy. Yet, this is still a normal requirement of all organizations and part of sound management. The important word is "reasonable." If you feel sabotaged, gutted, or totally shocked by what you hear, consider whether there is something deeper going on. If no path for improvement or performance plan is offered, this is another sign that bullying may be involved.

Unpopular, yet defensible decision-related management (i.e. resource allocation, solving budget problems, project scale reduction, and scheduling decisions that increase workload).

We easily get personally invested in our work. We lose sight of the broader strategic vision or priorities within our organizations. However, embracing change and agility is a hallmark of most successful organizations. When priorities, customer requirements, budgets, or management decisions negatively impact our work, it's easy to lash out when faced with our personal disappointment. While the decision may not be appreciated, as long as it's defensible and aligns with broader goals, we have to show maturity, flexibility, and capacity to adapt. However, if the decision is flavored with revenge, manipulation, sabotage, or personal humiliation, the possibility of bullying surfaces.

***

The key is to approach each situation with a reasonable, objective perspective in order to properly assess if there is bullying involved. Seek the advice from trusted colleagues or human resource specialists (but it is best not to ask those within your organization for help until you've received credible, unbiased advice). Ask experienced mentors who are outside of your workplace to provide their insight.

There may also be helpful tools within or external to your organization to help you evaluate the situation.

For example, as a certified project manager, I have access to the Project Management Institute's ethics tools and the five-step "Ethical Decision-Making Framework"[12] to assist in analyzing tough situations. I also have access to ethics and professional conduct resources through my law society. Perhaps your organization has an Employee Assistance Program that provides confidential professional resources to help you sort out a problem. Use these tools if you can.

> I find it's usually the bullies who are the
> most insecure.
>
> *Tom Felton*[13]

What Motivates the Bully?

Likely the second most common (and totally understandable) question is: "Why do bullies bully?" The answer lies in a complex web of jealousy, insecurity, and inadequacy wrapped in a blanket of narcissism and egoism.

Bullies target those who they fear will steal the attention away from them or those who they are envious of (usually because the target is highly regarded and popular – exactly what the bully isn't). In effect, that means if you are highly skilled, experienced, respected, and ethical, you represent a threat. The bully very purposefully selects the target and begins a campaign of undermining and destruction to ensure the threat is eliminated.

Following a militaristic command methodology, bullies generally approach their targets using fear, intimidation, and threats. Mark, a bullying target, described how afraid he was to speak up and that he felt he was working for a "workplace terrorist." This point of reference seems extreme, but it is one of the most accurate descriptions for bullies I have heard.

Bullies are malicious, arrogant, sneaky, and underhanded. They commonly treat people like children. They encourage conflict and, above all, they create a work environment rife with stress and fear. In short, it bears repeating – they are workplace terrorists.

Those of us who aren't psychologists or counselors tend to simplify what we see. We aren't trained to appreciate the complex web of personality issues underlying bullying behavior. One of the most common conclusions that we draw is that bullies rarely have any capacity to care or feel compassion (and that usually leaks into their personal lives). This isn't always true but it takes an experienced counselor, psychologist or social worker to figure that out. It is fair to say they are usually narcissistic and consumed by their ego. They are driven, at all costs, to prove themselves and disprove those around them to ensure they are in the limelight. They are control freaks and don't see any other perspective but their own. They hide their deep-rooted inadequacy in a shield and image of impenetrable power and ruthless wielding of authority.

There is a clear message that should anyone dare question or challenge their authority, the punishment will be swift and severe. For example, Kelly worked with a bully who proudly announced that someone who thought he had made a poor decision had been promptly fired. Job security is a very common threat used by bullies.

Bullies use their image of being cutthroat, powerful, and mean-spirited to their advantage as a scare tactic for submission. Sharon's bully actually took pleasure when introducing himself to new people, referencing that his reputation had likely preceded him (and he was proud of that).

In Joe's story about the bully in his life, Joe was punished for creating a team that "liked him." The bully actually noted that it was imperative that "subordinates fear you." That choice of words is quintessential bullying behavior.

Bullies also commonly make decisions that cross ethical boundaries and breach organizational policies. Bullies don't believe the rules apply to them and that in order to get the results that drive their ego, any tactic is acceptable. David's organization had very clear policies supporting work/life balance, families, and alternate work arrangements. Nonetheless, his bully manager refused to allow any women to work anything but an inflexible full-time schedule.

When approached with a situation relating to a very

short-term arrangement for an employee with a family chal-lenge, David's bully boss proudly noted that the predomi-nantly female team had no one working part-time and that it never would under his watch. He bluntly refused a reasonable request aligned perfectly with the organizational policies on principal, even noting that the employee's poor choice of fam-ily arrangement wasn't his or David's problem.

Finally, it is almost a given that the bully will have se-nior management under his/her charm and in his/her favor. Bullies are masters of political games and openly engage in self-promotion. Erica Pinsky's book titled *Road to Respect: Path to Profit* is helpful on this topic. She notes:

> *Typically, bullies are very clever and manipulative. The face they present to their own bosses is charming, solicit, and agreeable. Their managers usually view them as efficient, able to deal with touchy issues and situations, someone who gets results.[14]*

***

Therein lies our challenge. While ruining lives of the targets, bullies are pleasant, sycophantic, and manipulative to the executives, supervisors, and human resource personnel. A direct consequence of those perceived short-term "great re-sults" for which they always take credit are the many people left in the bully's wake, suffering untold physical and mental problems. Also, looking at the long-term, the financial, HR, employee turnover, team dysfunction, and stakeholder im-pacts resulting from a bully are potentially staggering – all of which will be discussed in other chapters.

The Prevalence of Workplace Bullying

Workplace bullying is everywhere, in every sector, work-force, and country – and the levels of its prevalence should send shivers of concern through any organizational leader. In a February 2015 article in the *Financial Post*, Ray Williams noted: "Workplace bullying has become a silent epidemic in North America, one that has huge hidden costs in terms of employee well-being and productivity."[15]

The percentage of people bullied will vary based on country, industry, gender, organizational culture, and many other factors. I have heard stories from targets, co-workers, managers, HR personnel, professionals, and executives around the world. However, rather than relying on anecdotal references, for this section, I have relied on the research and statistics of others.

> **Bullying is a national epidemic.**
>
> *Macklemore[16]*

To begin, according to a 2013 *Harvard Business Review* article, over the last few decades, the number of people who've admitted to being the target of workplace bullying has increased drastically.[17] The Workplace Bullying Institute conducted a 2014 survey on the prevalence of bullying in the workplace in the United States. The overall survey results are very clear (and quite shocking). Out of 1,000 people surveyed, 7 out of 10 workers are affected by workplace bullying. Twenty-seven percent responded that they have been or are currently being bullied.[18]

Other recent research indicates that the prevalence of bullying is even higher. Jennifer Grasz reports that 35% of the workforce is bullied.[19] According to Clare Rayner and Ståle Einarsen, both respected bullying researchers, 53%[20] of the workforce is bullied and even up to 75%[21] of the workforce is bullied. In a 2015 *Computer Weekly* article, a survey of 860

IT workers in the United Kingdom showed that 65% believed they had been bullied at work.[22]

***

The statistics are sobering. Bullies are prevalent and the harm they cause has direct impacts on people, workplace harmony, and profits/success. If there is a bully operating in your midst, the impact on the team will be toxic, which inevitably has negative broader impacts for the organization.

2

How to Identify a Bullying Situation

Good manners will open doors that the best education cannot.

— Clarence Thomas, Associate
Justice of the U.S. Supreme Court[1]

Rudeness/Competitiveness

What do you do if you have a difficult, aggressive boss? How can you manage an intensely competitive and rude colleague? Is it bullying, bad manners, or merely normal competition within a workplace? In order to be able to answer these questions it's important to have the objectivity and tools to contrast normal competitive work behavior with rudeness and bullying.

As a sad starting point, many would argue that bad manners are almost the norm in today's self-oriented, competitive world. Rudeness may be acceptable in some places. So you have to begin by setting the bar at a reasonable and appropriate place. Context is important and your analysis should begin from a starting place that aligns with the workplace culture. If you work at a place that is known for its cutthroat culture, then approach the review from this informed position.

Mohammed worked at a large technology company. He

was feeling beaten up and diminished. His boss regularly be-rated him and his team, using words like "idiots," "losers," and "morons." The team's work was never good enough. The ex-pectations were unreasonable and unattainable. At first, Mo-hammed concluded that his boss was a bully. However, upon objective reflection, he realized all managers in the compa-ny seemed to have this leadership style. It was a "survival of the fittest" workplace culture; Mohammed concluded that he was working in a Darwinian organization. The culture wasn't going to change. His boss was rude and demeaning, but he treated everyone like that.

These situations require introspection. It's very easy to say, "My boss Allen is a jerk." Allen may actually be a jerk – but perhaps you work in a highly competitive culture or one that doesn't prioritize politeness. That is what Mohammed discovered. In other words, observe the workplace culture in order to establish what is the norm.

Healthy competition and even some assertive challenge can make for a creative work environment where people push one another to better performance. This is very typical in high tech and other innovation-focused workplaces. Howev-er, some organizations turn competition into a fear and ridi-cule-based culture.

Once you have gained an objective appreciation for the workplace culture, you can analyze whether you are facing a bully or just an ill-mannered colleague. As a first step, when trying to discern the ethos of your workplace conflict, it is helpful to ask yourself whether you're being overly sensitive or misinterpreting the situation. Step back and look at the sit-uation, trying to separate emotion from the behavior. Person-al accountability is an effective filter and the situation is rarely one-sided. Self-evaluation can be tough. I suggest that you get a second opinion from someone you trust, who will tell you the truth, not just what you want to hear.

Once you have completed this assessment, it is

common that you've experienced bad manners and/or poor communication as a starting point. It is also possible that you may have contributed to the dysfunction. Regardless, the least effective means to resolve conflict is sitting back and doing nothing. Things won't resolve by themselves. The only way that your relationship will improve is by talking about it and respectfully engaging in a process to reason things out.

The next step is to formulate an appropriate engagement strategy. As a firm believer in self-improvement, I recommend that you hold yourself accountable for your contributions. A lot of positive results in conflict resolution begin after a sincere apology has been made. The next, and often difficult, step is to attempt to directly engage with the offender and explain that you don't appreciate being treated rudely.

Hopefully, she/he will also be accountable for her/his poor behavior and you can both move on with some new boundaries for behavior in place. If there are no amends made or behavior alterations, you may need to consider getting your manager or other influencers involved.

However, if you feel the behavior is more than rudeness, I recommend that you review the definition of bullying in order to evaluate whether you've got a much bigger problem on your hands. There is an objective and, in my opinion, clear line between rudeness and bullying. As already noted, the most important evaluation criteria are whether the behavior is repetitive, disrespectful, deliberate, and always for the bully's benefit. If you determine you are dealing with a bully, there are action plans provided in Chapter 7 to assist.

Harassment

Harassment means different things in different jurisdictions. It may have a more serious legal connotation or it may be what is commonly referred to as "unacceptable workplace behavior" as laid out in your organization's Respectful Workplace Policy. It is, therefore, important to understand the general meaning of the word "harassment" in your workplace and jurisdiction when comparing bullying to harassment.

As a lawyer, I prefer not to use the word "harassment" to describe disrespectful workplace behavior. For those of us in the legal profession, harassment historically connotes sexual misconduct within the context of a hostile work environment. Harassment has more narrow points of reference. It also has potentially criminal consequences that send legal alarm bells off. If you are the victim of sexual misconduct, my advice is to seek the assistance of the police and, if you feel it is needed, obtain legal advice. This is a serious matter that requires specially trained professionals and experts.

Regardless of my personal bias against the use of the word harassment, in some Western countries and organizations, "harassment" is synonymous with "unacceptable workplace behavior" as defined in many workplace respect policies. In such places, "harassment" has even replaced "unacceptable workplace behavior." For example, in Canada, the federal government's respectful workplace policy is actually called the Policy on Harassment Prevention and Resolution. Harassment is defined as:

> *Improper conduct by an individual, that is directed at and offensive to another individual in the workplace, including at any event or any location related to work, and that the individual knew or ought reasonably to have known would cause offence or harm. It comprises objectionable act(s), comment(s), or display(s) that demean, belittle, or cause personal humiliation or embarrassment, and any act of intimidation or threat.[2]*

This definition is very similar to the definition of "unacceptable workplace behavior" that is used in most respectful workplace policies, as you'll see in Chapter 3.

Provided you are dealing with a definition of "harassment" that is associated with a Respectful Workplace Policy, the same conclusions can be drawn. Bullying takes place in a disrespectful workplace and may look and feel like harassment within most of these policies. In this context, bullying is a clear violation of the policy against harassment with the same internal processes and challenges already discussed.

If, however, you live and work in a jurisdiction where harassment is a reference to potentially criminal behavior, and you feel that you are facing such a situation, seeking the advice of policing and legal professionals is best advised. See also the section on Discrimination in Chapter 4 for guidance.

Workplace Violence

Fortunately, it is very rare for a bully to resort to violence. While bullying is clearly the equivalent of psychological assault, it is highly unusual to result in or involve physical assault of the target. Bullies prefer to break a target's spirit rather than her bones.

One point that bears noting is the possibility that targets of bullying who have reached the end of their tolerance and capacity to think clearly may be more likely to act out. In an article at LiveScience.com, the stress that a target feels is described as follows:

> *This is why a person can't make quality decisions... They can't even consider alternatives. Just like a battered spouse, they don't even perceive alternatives to their situations when they're stressed and depressed and under attack.*[3]

When a target has been beaten down to the point of considering suicide, it is understandable that they might consider revenge or retribution against the bully or the leaders of the organization who the target thinks supported the bully. However, even in extreme cases, rather than respond with violence towards the bully, the victim is more likely to turn the violence inward, resulting in documented cases of target suicide.

***

Distinguishing bullying from rudeness, harassment, and workplace violence requires analysis. Review the definition of bullying and common behaviors. Consider your workplace culture. Assess your contributions to the situation, if any. These steps usually provide the clarity needed to decide what kind of behavior you are facing.

Bullying Isn't a "Leadership Style"

There is nothing that I find more distasteful than organizational attempts to diminish a bully's acts by describing them as a "leadership style." First, bullying is the opposite of leadership. Any reference to the contrary is simply untrue. Behavior that creates an intimidating or humiliating work environment can't possibly be leadership. Second, such inaccurate references indirectly support and condone the behavior. Third, those who are legitimate leaders have their skills marginalized when an executive equates true leadership to bullying.

> **Outstanding leaders go out of their way to boost the self-esteem of their personnel. If people believe in themselves, it's amazing what they can accomplish.**
>
> *Sam Walton, Co-Founder of Wal-Mart*[4]

For the sake of education, it's worth conducting an item-by-item comparison of the characteristics of leaders and bullies.

LEADERS	BULLIES
Encourage	Demotivate/dictate
Set good example	Disrupt/aggressive
Show integrity	Lack integrity
Demonstrate accountability	Avoid responsibility
Build	Destroy
Resolve conflict	Create conflict
Fair/mature	Unfair/immature

Leaders inspire and build functional teams. They value others, reward competence, and encourage contribution. They set good examples, holding themselves to the same high standards they expect of others. They aim for clarity. Behaving with maturity, they take responsibility for their mistakes. They let others work without interference. They resolve conflicts in fair, supportive ways.

By contrast, bullies erode and disrupt functional teams. They may use team language but they're not team players. They devalue others. They are threatened by the competence of others. They stifle contribution. They set bad examples and exhibit hypocrisy. They pollute the workplace by projecting their own negativity onto others, creating confusion and uncertainty. They lack integrity and maturity. They lie and blame others to disguise their own failings. They focus on petty fault finding. They generate conflict.

If you hear an executive describing a bully as a leader, my best advice is to take note and appreciate that the workplace culture supports bullying. Be careful about expressing your opposing opinion about the bully. It may make your situation worse.

The truth may be sobering but with knowledge comes the power to choose (if you can) to successfully initiate and implement an exit strategy to a more respectful and harmonious work environment.

> The purpose of human life is to serve, and to show compassion and the will to help others.
>
> *Albert Schweitzer[5]*

Who Are the Most Common Targets?

Unlike schoolyard bullying, people in the workplace are not targeted because they are perceived as loners, outcasts, different, or weak. Most likely, they are targeted because of their abilities, likeability, or other positive characteristics that may have posed a threat to the bully. The perception of threat is entirely in his/her mind, but it's what he/she feels and believes.

I believe that the most innovative, hardworking, and talented employees are often perceived as threats because they are drawing attention, accolades, and people toward their work – likely away from the bully or his/her projects.

Jonathan was one of the most respected and experienced employees in his unit. Until his boss was transferred into his unit, he also was a top performer, always ready to go beyond. He enjoyed complex projects and challenging himself to learn. He had received awards and accolades from every supervisor he had ever worked with. Then Ann arrived.

She quickly realized Jonathan was very bright, revered, and a star performer. She found this intimidating and instantly began her bullying campaign of interpersonal destruction against Jonathan, ruining his career and confidence.

The Workplace Bullying Institute's research findings from a 2000 study confirm that targets are usually veterans and the most highly skilled persons in the workgroup.[6] Common attributes of targets often include the following:

- Targets are independent.
- Targets are more technically skilled than their bullies.
- They are the "go-to" veteran workers to whom new employees turn for guidance.
- Targets are better liked.
- They have more social skills and, quite likely, possess greater emotional awareness and maturity.
- Colleagues, customers, and management appreciate the warmth that the targets bring to the workplace.
- Targets are ethical and honest.
- Targets are people with personalities founded on a nurturing and social orientation – a desire to help, heal, teach, develop, and nurture others.

**

The logic for eliminating a team member with such enviable skills and talent makes no sense unless you focus on the "enviable." Instead of rewarding the target for his/her exceptional contributions and assistance in helping the bully achieve results, targets are singled out for abuse and mistreatment. Bullies intentionally identify and take calculated steps to kill the target's reputation, spirit, and self-esteem, driving them from the workplace.

What Are the Most Common Bullying Scenarios?

Generally speaking, bullies most often target those underneath them in the organizational hierarchy. This translates into a simple fact – the majority of bullies are bosses. According to the Workplace Bullying Institute, 56% of bullies choose a subordinate as their target.[7] This is why the situation is so difficult for the target. If they complain, the natural and often effective response from the bully is that the target is a poor performer and using the complaint as a tactic to deflect attention away from this problem.

Being adept at deceit, bullies paint a very negative picture of the target that HR usually supports. HR then takes protective action in defense when one of their own is accused. This makes the odds of a fair and successful target complaint less than ideal.

> **Not everyone has been a bully or the victim of bullies, but everyone has seen bullying, and seeing it, has responded to it by joining in or objecting, by laughing or keeping silent, by feeling disgusted or feeling interested.**
>
> *Octavia E. Butler[8]*

Even more distressing is that in private and, if they feel they can be honest, invariably, human resource personnel will admit that the boss is a bully (or at least they wouldn't want to work for her/him). Often they also feel like they have been "told" what to do by the bully and feel intimidated. The bully usually has friends in high places and HR feels pressure to fall in line.

Susan shared her bullying story beginning with a startling comment – "We just fired the second bully vice president in two years." While she wasn't the target, she worked in a role that allowed her to observe from a distance. Her experience with HR was what concerned her the most. Not only did they protect the bullies at first, they created plans to deal with the targets instead of the bullies. They believed the targets were a bigger risk to the company than the bullies. Fearing lawsuits, sabotage, sick leave claims, and public relations problems, HR empowered the bullies.

Susan had the chance to discuss the situation with a senior HR member after the second bully was fired. Her colleague not only admitted that she was fully aware that the vice presidents were bullies, but also that she feared she would become a target if she didn't support them.

Susan was astonished – when replacing the first bully with his mentor, the company failed to consider the obvious. Bully Gordon was replaced by Bully Jessica who learned all she needed to know about how to succeed as a bully from Gordon. While the company eventually solved the real problem, it took them two vice presidents and enormous resources to eliminate the bullies and reset the workplace culture.

Bullies take on colleagues about one third of the time. The bully perceives a coworker as competition, perhaps for a promotion. It's the same game, just with a different person in the crosshairs.

Very rarely does a "bully up," taking on someone of higher rank. Instead, they apply their manipulative social skill, ensuring those above protect them. They simply focus on "getting those outstanding results" and "taking care of the problems no one else seems to be able to solve." By ingratiating themselves, bullies ensure they are virtually untouchable (at least that is how they view it).

***

Most of the time, the bully is your boss or supervisor. This dynamic creates a challenging environment for targets, co-workers, and teams, both for coping with and for complaining about the bully.

However, there are many practical tools that you have in your Anti-bullying Toolkit to help you cope. We will discuss ways to manage and even confront the problem in Chapter 7, with action plans for everyone impacted by bullying.

3

How Does My Organization Deal with Bullying?

Willingness to change is a strength, even if it means plunging part of the company into total confusion for a while.

— Jack Welch[1]

Many of us don't know where to begin when we are faced with a bullying situation. Once you're certain you are dealing with a bully, the next step is to determine what your organization has done, if anything, to prevent or prohibit bullying.

In order to begin to determine how (if at all) your organization and workplace bullying intersect, the first place to search is for any workplace behavior policies. Take time to investigate. This investigation will determine what options are available to address the problem. It will also impact your action plan goals.

In most large, multi-national and governmental organizations, bullying falls into the broader language of a Workplace Respect Policy that stipulates what is unacceptable workplace behavior. As discussed in more detail in the previous chapter, most policies provide a broad definition of what is considered unacceptable behavior. Usually the definition contains wording like the following:

> *Systematic, annoying, and continued actions that include threats and demands; creating a hostile work situation by uninvited and unwelcome verbal or physical conduct.*

There is no doubt that bullying could fall within the definition of most organizational workplace respect policies. Bullying takes place in a disrespectful workplace and may look and feel like harassment within most of these policies.

Workplace respect policies also provide mechanisms and processes for addressing behavior that violates the policy. They usually have some form of formal complaint process. Reviewing these processes and researching their effectiveness is also helpful. Find out how other complaints have been resolved. The more historical information you have, the better able you are to evaluate your bullying problem. You'll know the risks and rewards of complaining. It will inform you and help you craft your action plan.

> **To be one, to be united is a great thing. But to respect the right to be different is maybe even greater.**
>
> *Bono[2]*

One note of warning – in many organizations it isn't obvious that bullying is unacceptable because there isn't a clear policy stating so. Given the overwhelming evidence about the serious impacts caused by bullies, it is difficult to understand why some organizations fail to implement workplace respect policies with clear references to bullying. I would even argue it is negligent. Nonetheless, many people work in places that have failed to grasp the business sense of anti-bullying policies.

Instead of naming it "bullying," some organizations prefer to use more neutral terms. They are shy to give workplace bullying such a direct identifier. I can understand this, but it doesn't help prevent and address the issue when you water it down using less impactful or grey terminology.

With that in mind, I've seen organizations encapsulate bullying behavior within a variety of terms including "workplace disrespect," "unacceptable workplace behavior," "workplace harassment," and "rudeness." While it may not be ideal, it is still much better than having no behavioral guidelines at all.

Finally, there is the worst-case scenario – organizations that fail to even bother with any policy guiding workplace behavior at all. Leaving such a critical component of workplace culture to develop without any guidelines is highly risky and, in my opinion, foolish. An inclusive, respectful workplace culture is essential for employee engagement and motivation. Leaving such a driver for innovation and performance to chance is negligent and just plain bad for business.

Such organizations also make it almost impossible for both the organization and its employees to take effective action against a bully (or any other bad behavior). Without anything in writing to reference what is acceptable behavior, the workplace is basically a behavioral free-for-all. Such organizations are perfect environments for work terrorists – with no accountability structure in place, the workplace is their oyster.

If your organization has behavioral rules in place, dig deeper. Review what the process is for complaining. Research what the historical complaint results have been. Find out if other bullying complaints have been made and what happened. All of this information will help in the action plan decision-making process discussed in detail later on.

If you work in an organization without such policies, the challenges you face when seeking assistance from your organization or attempting to motivate management to take action are very serious. It is essential to be realistic and objectively weigh the likelihood of achieving a positive result from reporting the bully.

***

With the results of your investigation into your organization's workplace behavior policy in hand, you have completed the first step in the process. Now, you can begin to plan your next move. Options to consider are discussed later on.

Bullying and Respectful Workplace Policies

As already noted, many organizations have some form of Respectful Workplace Policy or Expected Guidelines for Employee Behavior. Most policies provide a broad definition of what is considered unacceptable behavior. Bullying is usually a policy violation, at least on paper.

I applaud any organization that sets down guidelines for unacceptable workplace behavior. However, organizations must consistently and assertively apply the policy. They must respond fairly and effectively to violation allegations. Complaints can't be shrugged off lightly or interpreted as two employees that can't get along.

In other words, the leaders must "walk the walk" and follow through by demonstrating that the policy is valued and enforced. I've heard many hollow clichés about organizations that allegedly view their employees as their most valuable asset yet do nothing when it comes to demonstrating real leadership in the case of workplace bullies.

Sharon told me her government department had a very clear and strongly worded workplace respect policy. It even referenced bullying directly. Her bully had been with the organization for over a decade and everyone working there knew about her boss's well-deserved reputation as a bully. However, when she filed a very carefully, well-documented bullying complaint, she was treated as if she was a trouble-maker. She was labeled as the problem – the human resources manager promptly informed the boss, leading to an intolerable escalation of bullying. Sharon ended up having a heart attack. Thankfully, she recovered and left the organization. Those left behind were also devastated and, one by one, everyone who could, moved on to more harmonious places. So much for that respectful workplace policy!

As evidenced by Sharon's experience, it is also import-ant to appreciate that workplace respect policies are internal to organizations. Therefore, if an employee is accused of vio-lating the policy, it is managed exclusively from within. Any investigation, resolution, or punishment is a corporate affair. This further underlines why it is important to send consistent and clear messaging to all staff and follow through.

The internal reality of workplace respect policies also highlights their weakness. The vast majority of executives and managers are afraid to engage the bully in a confrontation about their behavior. They also lack awareness and training in how to successfully approach the problem. Furthermore, they fail to consult with experts that they can turn to for advice. These valuable subject matter experts are readily available to help strategically intervene.

In most organizations, the human resource staff and managers lack training or skills for dealing with bullies. When management turns to them for help, they regularly provide unhelpful recommendations. They believe influencers can reason with a bully and that once they have expressed their concerns, things will improve. Experts in bullying intervention confirm this is often ineffective.

Furthermore, as will be discussed in other chapters, normal complaint, investigation, and conflict-resolution processes used in most organizations aren't effective with bullies. The most common complaint process directs employees to lodge a complaint with their supervisor. When bullies are the bosses most of the time, it's easy to see why this fails to resolve the problem.

Without the appropriate specialized training and procedures, targets that complain usually get little satisfaction from the matter. Although it is entirely preventable, the internal system is stacked against effective resolution.

***

Despite their good intentions and best efforts, many organizations fail to protect themselves and their employees when they initiate respectful workplace policies and programs. The bullies use their talent for manipulation, deceit, and counter-attack to turn the process into another opportunity to bully. Chapter 6 examines ways that organizations can take charge in a bullying situation and protect not only the bottom line but the integrity of the organization.

4

Is Workplace Bullying Illegal?

I find hope in the darkest of days, and focus in the brightest. I do not judge the universe.
— Dalai Lama[1]

"Is workplace bullying illegal?" This is a question that I often get asked and, like many legal questions, the best answer is: "It depends." It depends mostly on where you live and whether there is human rights or anti-workplace bullying legislation in place.

Bullying potentially violates the law if it is proven that the bullying falls within the clearly defined terms of the legislation. It is best to seek the help of legal professionals and other relevant authorities in your area if you are facing a bullying situation that might fall within the terms of applicable legislation. Each type of legislation is described separately.

Discrimination

Most countries have state (or province) and federal civil rights laws that are designed to protect workers from discriminatory and disparate mistreatment (commonly referred to in legal terms as "discriminatory workplace harassment"). Discriminatory workplace harassment enters the domain of human rights law and becomes quite technical.

If, and only if, you are a member of a protected status group and you have been mistreated by a person at work (the bully) who is not a member of a protected group might you be able to claim that you were a victim of discriminatory workplace harassment. This confusing statement requires an explanation absent legal jargon.

Discriminatory workplace harassment has a legal foundation that is different from workplace bullying. It is much more narrow than behaviors captured by a workplace respect policy. While many employers have policies that prohibit bullying-type behavior, these are separate from the issue of discrimination. Erica Pinsky, in her book titled *Road to Respect: Path to Profit*, notes:

> [Discriminatory] Workplace harassment flows from human rights law...and is very specifically defined...Human rights law was structured in response to historical discrimination in our society.[2]

In order for an individual to be deemed to be illegally harassing another at work, the victim must be able to prove that they were targeted for their race, gender, age, religion, ethnicity, marital status, sexual orientation, or another ground noted in the law. Only then can the behavior be potentially categorized as a form of illegal discrimination that can be defined as:

> A type of discrimination and means engaging in a course of annoying comments or conduct that is known or ought reasonably to be known to be unwelcome, that is tied to a prohibited ground of discrimination and that detrimentally affects the work environment or leads to adverse job-related consequences for the victim of harassment.[3]

In order for the possibility of discriminatory workplace

harassment to be involved, there must first be human rights legislation in effect. Second, the bully must be engaging in conduct that is directed to a person in a way that violates what is best described as a prohibited ground of discrimination as provided by the law (i.e. religion, color, sexual orientation, etc.).

Generally, most bullying is "status-blind" harassment. In other words, the bully isn't targeting the victim because she is Asian, Christian, pregnant, gay, or some other identifying trait that is protected by law from discrimination. However, it is estimated that in about 20% of the cases, there is a link between bullying and discrimination.

> *Life comes from physical survival; but the good life comes from what we care about.*
>
> Rollo May[4]

For example, let's assume you live in England. The United Kingdom has enacted human rights legislation that declares it illegal to discriminate against anyone on the basis of religion. If a workplace bully targets a person because he is a Muslim and there is proof that his religion was the basis for bullying, then there is the possibility that the bullying is illegal discrimination. If this line has been crossed, there is a chance that the bully could be criminally charged with discriminatory workplace harassment.

The main difference between discriminatory workplace harassment and "normal" workplace bullying is that this is a matter for the legal professionals and authorities to handle. Also, the potential outcomes are a lot more significant. Unlike violations of workplace respect policies, allegations of discrimination are external to an organization and potentially involve serious consequences for the bully if proven and convicted.

In addition, this severe type of bullying would also undoubtedly represent a breach of an organization's workplace respect policy. Thus, it is possible that a bully could be both externally and internally investigated and punished for her actions.

Workplace Bullying Laws

There is a clear legislative trend to make workplace bullying illegal (usually as a health and workplace safety issue). However, this is very much still evolving in many parts of the world. At the moment, the world leaders on the anti-bullying law front are the European Union (with France in the lead), Australia, the United Kingdom, Canada, and New Zealand. All of the countries represented have passed anti-workplace bullying legislation (or the states/provinces that have the legal authority in this domain have done so).

The United States still has no national anti-workplace bullying legislation, although one is being proposed and slowly moving through the political processes. As of the date of publication, twenty-nine states and two territories have introduced the anti-bullying Healthy Workplace Bill which, when it becomes law, will radically change the face of workplace bullying in the United States. There is some very interesting media coverage in the U.S. about the anti-bullying bills that have been introduced in many states thus far. For those interested, YouTube has some helpful video materials.

If you are fortunate and live in a place that has passed laws making workplace bullying illegal, then you have the luxury of a second layer of protection that is external to the policies of your organization. Generally speaking, once such legislation is passed, organizations are forced to take real action. They often implement much stronger policies, training initiatives, and procedures for handling bullying complaints, investigations, and resolution.

While they are cumbersome and bureaucratic, even the possibility of an external investigation, publicity, and legal violation is a major motivator for organizations to address workplace bullying in a meaningful way.

If, on the other hand, no such legislation exists, then you are unfortunately left with internal processes as your only "official" recourse. Sadly, billions of workers in the world fall into this category. Even more depressing is the fact that many organizations in the developing world have yet to establish workplace respect policies.

***

Workplace bullying can be illegal. However, much depends on interpretations of the laws in place (assuming there are any). Get help from experts if you believe the bullying violates the applicable legislation in your country, state, or province.

Government Response to Workplace Bullying

In many countries, increased public awareness and research have paved the way for recognition of bullying as a workplace hazard. In effect, the impacts of bullying are considered a risk to worker safety. Once legislators began to appreciate the mental and physical health impacts of bullying, they started to take action to create laws that make it illegal.

As previously noted, many Western countries have wholly embraced legislation and others are moving in that direction. The message that bullying is costly to society (healthcare, disability, unemployment payments, etc.) and bad for business may very well be the most effective lobbying tactic to persuade other governments to follow suit. The greater the awareness, the more likely governments will take action.

It bears noting though that even when there is legislation in effect, that doesn't mean bullying stops. While it certainly is a grand step in the right direction, bullying won't stop until every organization takes bold and unwavering action to make it stop. Governments can help but they aren't the panacea. Grassroots motivation to change is always more effective.

In order to determine if your country, province, or state has made workplace bullying illegal, consult with a local human resources, legal, or government experts.

***

There is an undeniable movement towards illegalizing workplace bullying. Government engagement is tremendously helpful and can't be understated. However, governments alone can't resolve the problem. The true test of success is how deeply embraced the change is throughout society. Each one of us can be a change management leader.

5

Bullying Is Bad for Business

The great aim of education is not knowledge but action.

— Herbert Spencer[1]

As previously noted, the impacts of bullying are widespread and significant. In order to make sense of the depth and breadth of the types of impact, the diagram on page 42 is helpful. I view bullying through a pyramidal lens with the targets forming the foundation and the layers of other people and types of impacts rising above. The pyramid is designed with a purpose.

Many business leaders would likely say that bullying is wrong, but not all recognize that it has tangible and significant organizational costs or where those costs and impacts are felt. I firmly believe that the key to eradicating workplace bullying is with education. Once organizations solidly appreciate how one bully's actions can permeate throughout the workplace, causing extraordinary impacts, workplace bullying will cease.

In order to respond to a skeptical executive, politician, or senior manager, it helps to have clear information about each cost/impact. Use the information to tailor-make an approach to focus on the areas about which the influencer is most concerned. By putting ourselves in the world of the leaders, modeling the conversation on identifying topics or statistics that resonate in their world, I believe we can influence change. Hopefully, we can keep them up at night until they take real action.

The pyramid shows the escalation of impacts on organizations and drives the lesson in awareness. As each layer is revealed, objective and persuasive evidence mounts. Costs/impacts caused by bullies can be categorized and analyzed into a series of buckets, each having potentially more significant impact.

Regardless of where we fit in the organizational hierarchy, as sad as it may seem, I believe we need to see "what's in it for me" in order to be motivated to change. Once everyone is on the same page, armed with their own reasons for embracing an anti-bullying agenda, only then will organizational behavior change. It clearly helps if leaders set the example – but there also needs to be individual accountability and motivation. I hope the pyramid provides information that acts as a motivational catalyst for change for everyone. Particularly as we reach the top levels of the structure, I believe that leaders will fully comprehend that bullies are simply bad for business, regardless of what business they are in.

The following is an analysis of each one of the pyramidal layers.

a) Targets

Targets of bullying face terrible impacts. Narrowing our impact discussion to the lives of targets is a sobering reality check. There are many documented negative health impacts that can be attributed to bullying. These impacts often slowly creep up, likely due to prolonged stress experienced by targets that deteriorate their physical or mental health.

Unfortunately, most targeted people try to "tough it out." This rarely stops the bullying and it allows the overwhelming stress to build. The stress will not end until the bullying ceases or the target is separated from the source of the stressors – the bully and the organization condoning him/her.

Bullying affects both the brain and body. I have broken the discussion of the health impacts of bullying into two categories: physical injuries and psychological injuries.

Physical Injuries

Stress-related diseases and health complications from prolonged exposure to the stressors of bullying that have been reported include but are not limited to:

- Cardiovascular impacts: heart attacks, hypertension, strokes
- Gastrointestinal problems: irritable bowel syndrome, colitis

- Infections
- Auto-immune disorders: fibromyalgia, chronic fatigue syndrome
- Diabetes
- Skin disorders

Psychological-Emotional-Mental Injuries

There is no better description of the mental impact of bullying than the following:

> *Bullying is often called psychological harassment or violence. What makes it psychological is its impact on the person's mental health and sense of well-being. The personalized, focused nature of the assault destabilizes and disassembles the target's identity, ego, strength, and ability to rebound from the assaults. The longer the exposure to stressors like bullying, the more severe the psychological impact upon the target.[2]*

Psychological injuries caused by bullying include:

- Debilitating anxiety
- Panic attacks
- Clinical depression
- Post-traumatic stress (PTSD)
- Suicide

The source of the health information above is the Workplace Bullying Institute's 2012 Impact on Employee Health Survey.[3]

Targets of bullying also routinely respond to the abuse, usually in a fashion that harms the organization rather than the bully. These impacts can have unexpected consequences for the employer. For example, through a poll conducted by the Workplace Bullying Institute[4] of 800 managers and employees in 17 industries, targets reported as follows:

Among workers who've been on the receiving end of bullying:

•48% intentionally decreased their work effort

•47% intentionally decreased the time spent at work

•38% intentionally decreased the quality of their work

•63% lost work time avoiding the offender

•66% said their performance declined

•12% said they left their job

These results align with the many stories that targets have shared with me and with my personal experience. As the bully's attack intensifies, the target's commitment to their work diminishes. They often punish their offenders and the organization. This information alone should send a chill up any senior manager's spine. Anything that can harm productivity and program success is worth looking at more closely.

b) Coworkers/Colleagues

Coworkers often suffer some of the same physical and mental impacts that targets do as a result of their direct engagement with both the bully and the target. They are caught in the web of chaos and find work a place of conflict, distress, and discomfort.

Coworkers also struggle emotionally, experiencing stress observing the bully. They also worry about the impacts on both themselves and their colleagues. They spend energy, caught in the middle and torn between supporting the target and protecting themselves from the bully. They take more stress and sick days than happy employees. They regularly look for work in a more harmonious organization.

Luis told me that he felt powerless, guilty, and afraid every day at work. He watched his coworker being bullied and was immobilized by fear of becoming the target. He did nothing. He felt awful. He found another job, but two years after leaving he still was carrying around the burden of "failing to take action."

c) Teams/Units

Bullying creates a toxic and stressful work environment for all those who work with the bully, regardless of who is the target. Productivity, performance, creativity, and team spirit deteriorate. Bullies prevent work from getting done, causing confusion and a loss of focus. Most executives will give their ear if you ask to talk about an issue related to productivity.

In a 2014 *Guardian Newspaper* article on the problems created by workplace bullying, writer Ian Erickson discussed how workplace bullying harms teams. He noted that:

> *Bullying...is behaviour that prevents work from being finished. Losses are caused by staff members struggling to cope at work, high rates of absenteeism and talented employees leaving in favour of a more harmonious place of employment.*[5]

Experiments and other reports offer additional insights about the effects of bullying. Not unexpectedly, they highlight that team and individual creativity suffer, team performance decreases and team spirit fades.

There is also a lost opportunity cost that can be quantified. That means that when the more talented target is driven from work, either through termination, constructive discharge, or quitting, the company loses the value that worker created. Further, the demotivated and stressed-out team that is left behind rarely recovers. Synergy, team commitment, and high performance are vital to success. Once that has been lost, particularly in a traumatic bullying drama, most teams fail to re-engage.

d) Programs/Projects

Virtually every organizational output is produced through a structured program or project. Having had the honor of many speaking presentations to global project, program, and portfolio professionals on the topic of bullying in project management, I've heard firsthand the stories of many failures, delays, and costs associated with bullies. Projects are subsets of workplaces and since project and program management is, for the most part, an activity that involves working very closely with others, the impact of a bully in a program or project is potentially lethal to success.

The workplace culture in many projects is pressure-filled and challenged by time, budget, and scope restraints. Many projects are competing for attention, priority, and resources. This is a perfect environment for a bully to use tactics to eliminate the perceived competition and take all the glory for any project successes.

Since the target is usually a "go-to veteran," the bully creates a talent vacuum where the best workers effectively cease engagement. You can imagine how that impacts the completion of the work itself. Unfortunately, bullies have a myopic view of the world and are unable to see they are effectively self-sabotaging.

Further, program/project managers rarely have enough positional authority to carry out their responsibilities. Most projects also occur in organizations where project team members report not only to the project manager but to a line manager as well. Consequently, they must increasingly rely on other indirect methods to motivate team members to accomplish the needed project work. The most effective of these other methods is by forming relationships with team members and influencers. Once again, that is precisely the kind of situation bullies can exploit.

In summary, bullies have deep and direct negative impacts on programs and projects. The division, demotivation, and confusion they create reduce innovation, engagement, and productivity. Finally, with the most experienced team motivators sidelined, many projects suffer financially and delays are commonplace. Simply put – bullies prevent work from getting done.

e) Organizations

As the "single most preventable and needless expense on a company's register" bullying is harmful to business productivity and workplace harmony. If commitments aren't fulfilled on time, budget, or scope, the impact ripples throughout the organization. Ending bullying is just plain good for business.

We've already touched upon how bullying impacts performance and productivity with self-evident results. We've also touched upon how bullies create a conflict-filled and disagreeable workplace culture. Without workplace harmony, further impacts occur that are most often seen by the human resources team.

For example, there is a direct link between bullying and sick-leave/disability claims. The stress and health impacts caused by bullying affect not only profits when your top talent takes time off work, but also requires the engagement of HR personnel to manage each situation. Bullied people (and their coworkers) often end up quitting for one reason or another. This has a significant negative impact on success, especially when the organization has to replace the best and brightest (the bullied ones and their coworkers).

Employee turnover costs are incurred and include employer contributions to retirement plans for the departed worker, head hunter/recruiting firm fees, time spent by managers and HR staff, hiring bonuses/incentives, and the harder-to-calculate lost production during the entire process that must be made up by coworkers.

The first place HR often turns to for advice is legal professionals. Time spent risk managing, strategizing, and preparing to respond with lawyers involved add up quickly. It is becoming more common for targets to turn to legal recourse to solve the problem, costing enormous amounts of time, stress, and money.

Further, courts are becoming more aware of workplace bullying with expected negative results for the companies that are found to have condoned the bully. Finally, severance costs regularly factor in. All tolled, a single bully can cause hundreds of thousands and even millions of dollars in costs if just one well-founded claim is successful, even before the matter gets anywhere near a court.

It is incredible what one bully can do to even a multi-billion dollar enterprise. Carl shared his story of the estimated costs that a bullying manager caused his company. Focusing exclusively on quantifying the impacts, he estimated that the direct loss was over a million dollars. Adding up the cost of the bullying investigation, experts, legal fees, severance costs, talent departure, sick leave, and HR time, the organization was left holding a seven-figure bill. To add salt to the wound, the bully they protected left the company within weeks of the "resolution" of the matter.

f) Reputation

Under the heading of reputation, there are two very different impacts to consider. The first, and most obvious, is the potential impact on the organization's reputation in the eyes of the world and their stakeholders. In 2015, the world witnessed Volkswagen's meteoric fall from grace losing billions of euros in share value and potentially jeopardizing the corporation's future. All thanks to a decision somewhere within the organization to choose to falsely improve emission results using a deviant piece of technology.

The world instantly and fittingly responded. Shame was heaped on the company because they chose profits over ethics. This is a terrific lesson and wake-up call for all organizations and plays perfectly into the issue of workplace bullying.

The 2015 media frenzy about the alleged Darwinian work environment at Amazon proves that bullying can have serious impacts on organizational reputation. If your workplace is perceived as toxic, people inevitably gossip about it. They share their frustration with anyone willing to listen, which, in the case of Amazon, led to journalist engagement from the *New York Times*.[6] Think of what such an event costs in public relations, communications, and lost time – a reputational event of Titanic proportions.

People are less likely to do business with a company harboring a bully, even if the bullying isn't directed at them. All they have to see or even hear about is the bully treating staff poorly. Disrespectful behavior makes people uncomfortable. People will judge organizations harshly. The tide is definitely turning towards a marketplace that is aware of the impacts of workplace bullying and won't support organizations that don't get on board.

The second aspect of reputation relates to the personal reputation of the executives that condone a bullying workplace culture. Almost every executive is (or should be) concerned about their own reputation as leaders, success-drivers, and model citizens. Leaders are judged by their actions and their values. Organizational leaders may find their own integrity at risk by protecting or failing to address bullying. Respect, trust, and loyalty are earned – a bully can ruin years of work building these values.

While it is acknowledged that some well-known leaders seem impervious to this concern, if you look a little closer, you may find they are bullies themselves. Are they actual devils wearing Prada? There are very few organizational leaders that would be insulated from the possibility of termination if faced with a Volkswagen "cheat device" event. Leaders beware – your reputation and job security could be at stake if you fail to address your workplace bullies.

g) Profits and Share Value

At the top of the pyramid in terms of issues that every senior executive worries about are profit and share value. There are direct negative and financial impacts that bullying has on the bottom line. Our challenge is pushing organizations to revise their focus on short-term results (which bullies are experts at achieving) to take a longer-term approach.

Getting the attention of senior management is never easy but one thing helps – cold, clear facts that objectify the problem and highlight the opportunity cost of not resolving it. In order to convince the skeptics, it may help to have some reliable data to shore up the argument that bullying is bad for business.

As already noted, in his 2014 *Guardian* article on the problems created by workplace bullying, writer Ian Erickson, references an article in which New Zealander Shane Cowishlaw writes that workplace bullying costs his country hundreds of millions of dollars.[7] Australia reports losses in the billions. Not surprisingly for organizations in the much larger United States, workplace bullying-related costs are estimated to be over $200 billion.

It bears noting the potential impact that a bullying workplace environment can have on share price. Again, using Amazon as a wonderful illustration of market forces at work, Amazon's share price dropped from $535.22 a share on August 17, 2015 (when the *New York Times* article was published) to $463.37 one week later. If that doesn't get executives sweating, then I don't know what might.

***

The impacts of bullying are widespread and significant. Viewing bullying through a pyramidal lens with the targets forming the foundation and the layers of other people and types of impacts rising above helps makes sense of it all. If organizations begin to recognize how bullies' actions ripple throughout the workplace, I believe bullying will be eliminated.

6

Employer Responsibility

If you are neutral in situations of injustice, you have chosen the side of the oppressor. If an elephant has its foot on the tail of a mouse, and you say that you are neutral, the mouse will not appreciate your neutrality.

— Desmond Tutu, South Africa[1]

I believe that employers have both a moral and ethical responsibility to take action. If they remain neutral, bullying will continue. If employers refuse to tolerate bullying in the workplace, it will stop – simple as that.

Regardless of what governments do, the real power to eliminate workplace bullying lies in the hands of employers. In simple terms, employers control and define all work conditions and policies of the workplace. They choose the strategies, values, and workplace behavior expectations. So, bullying – the system – can only be sustained or eliminated by employers.

Everyone within an organization can play an anti-bullying advocate role to encourage change. Furthermore, the public as consumers and concerned citizens can also take action by voting with their wallets and ballots. The power of shareholders and voters should never be underestimated.

Over time, there will be fewer Amazon stories, fewer organizations ruled by bullies, and more stories about exemplary employers.

Stopping bullying requires nothing less than turning the workplace culture upside down. Bullies must experience negative consequences for harming others. Punishment must replace promotions. Only executives and senior management can reverse the historical trend. To stop bullying requires employers to change the routine ways of "doing business" that have propped up bullies for years.

***

The ultimate responsibility for both the cause and cure for bullying rest squarely on the shoulders of senior management and executives. They put people in harm's way and they can provide safety by undoing the culture that allowed bullying to flourish.

Why Are Organizations So Ineffective at Managing Bullying?

Bullying is sufficiently understood and prevalent that most employers should be prepared to effectively handle it. However, despite laws, irrefutable data and research, and ethical reasons to do so, most organizations are generally very unprepared. They haven't yet come to appreciate the costs of not acting or the most effective ways to confront the problem. Senior management say "People are our most valuable asset," but that is often a hollow cliché when it comes to bullying.

> **Management is doing things right; leadership is doing the right things.**
>
> *Peter Drucker[2]*

Zogby Analytics was commissioned to conduct an online survey of 315 U.S. business leaders in three market areas: San Francisco, New York City, and Washington D.C. The survey was completed January 21, 2013.[3] The leaders were asked the following question:

> *Which of the following best describes your opinion of "workplace bullying"?*

The answers were enlightening. The percentages for each response option were:

> *68% agreed - It is a serious problem.*
>
> *17% answered - I have never heard of it.*
>
> *15% said - It is irrelevant, a non-issue, bullying affects only children.*

If so many business leaders think bullying is a serious problem, why are most organizations terrible at managing it? There are many contributors to fully answer this question. Often more than one factor is involved. It helps to identify the most common reasons. They include the following:

A Focus on Results

In our hyper-competitive world there are intense and ever-present demands for results. Many organizations become so focused on short-term results that they ignore how they are achieved or the long-term impacts of the means used to get those results. Organizations willingly sacrifice a harmonious workplace culture in order to please shareholders, customers, and stakeholders with baseline results. They may believe their employees matter most but in actual fact, results trump everything.

Sadly, this focal point is candy for bullies. If there is one commonality amongst bullies, it's a gift for whipping up results (and those used to get them). Later on, when organizations see the fallout from the bully, they realize that the price they paid for those results far exceeds the benefits reaped from them.

Through increased awareness and focusing on the costs associated with bullying, there is hope that even when faced with pressure to perform, organizations will forbid bullying as a results-driver. In the meantime, the stories of bullying will continue.

Misinterpretation of a "Competitive Workplace"

Many organizations confuse healthy competition with a "survival of the fittest" model for workplace behavior. High tech is infamous for condoning bullying, viewing it as normal behavior in a competitive workplace. There have been stories (and articles, books, and movies) about Amazon, Apple, and other companies where staff is regularly challenged to out-perform and out-innovate their colleagues using draconian rewards for the winner.

Some argue bullies manage these organizations, which is why the workplace culture is so Darwinian (an entirely reasonable assertion). To quote Orrin Woodward, founder of Life Leadership and bestselling author: "You cannot expect your team to rise above your example."[4]

If we assume that the CEO isn't a bully, I believe there is a lack of appreciation of the direct relationship between employee engagement and workplace culture. If there are rewards for cutthroat competition and the workplace culture resembles the set of the TV reality series *Survivor*, there is little chance for workplace respect. Bullies will thrive and there will be very little employee loyalty and engagement.

It is my hypothesis that leaders fail to understand that it is possible (and in the best long-term organizational interest) to have both workplace respect and healthy competition. Staff don't need to be abused to perform to their fullest.

A Belief that Bullying Is a Leadership Style

This false connection has already been discussed in a previous chapter. Bullying is the opposite of leadership. In my opinion, executives that use this excuse to support a bully are likely in denial or afraid to confront the problem. If asked in a moment of unbridled honesty, they likely know exactly who the abusers are. They just don't have the skills or motivation to take action so they leave the mess alone, hoping it will sort itself out. They discount the level of the problem, rationalize it as a temporary issue, blame it on a very challenging time, or find another excuse to avoid actively engaging.

A Lack of Awareness

As hard as it seems to accept, there remains a small segment of leadership that has yet to become enlightened on the topic of workplace bullying. What's even more surprising is that their ignorance may be genuine. Rather than judge the poorly informed, it may be more useful to see their lack of awareness as an opportunity to empower them with knowledge. If they are simply acting out of willful blindness, there is a lack of leadership at the core of the problem.

Employers Are Afraid to Confront Bullies

While most leaders are aware of workplace bullying and that it is a severe problem, many organizations lack the training, tools, policies, and expertise to confront it. More importantly, they are afraid to step into the ring with the bully. Bullying is a sensitive topic because it requires confrontation, conflict, and courage as much as it requires tools.

Fear often feeds into the ignorance: fear of lawsuits, of the actual confrontation with the bully, of what else might be uncovered once an investigation is launched, of how many other victims might be in the organization. Having talked with plenty of executives and HR personnel, it is fair to state that fear of conflict is a serious impediment to eliminating bullying. The result is that management walks on eggshells and is afraid to confront the "golden" bully. While HR does its best to deal with the complaints, conflicts, and impacts, the result is paralysis – and so the bullying continues.

However, there is a lost opportunity cost of doing nothing and, as has already been discussed, that cost is dear. Performance, productivity, and other ripple effects resonate throughout the organization. The bully continues to wreak havoc and this won't stop until the organization takes action – to get the guts to confront the bully. Remembering there are bully intervention experts who can effectively handle these difficult situations may help executives realize they don't have to take on the bully personally. Leave it to the outside, unbiased, and specially trained experts.

Lack of Effective Policies and Processes

It is remarkable how few organizations actually have taken all the evidence, information, and advice of experts about workplace bullying to heart. Whatever the reason for their inaction, there is a lack of effective policies and processes for dealing with bullying. For example, without a workplace respect policy (or similar), it is very difficult to frame the approach to address a bullying situation. On the other hand, if the organization has a robustly worded policy, the base from which to respond to a bully is well-founded.

Not only are the policies essential, but also the processes for actually managing bullying issues. Without a fair, impartial, confidential, and effective complaints process, the policy is meaningless. How does an organization expect to deal properly with bullying if the complaint process requires a formal written complaint to the supervisor? Lest we forget that bullies are statistically most often the supervisor to whom the complaint would have to be made. It is also helpful to remember that no alleged bully should be presumed guilty without due process. Thus, the process is essential to defensible and trustworthy outcomes.

Further, it is equally difficult if the human resources department is considered the best place for the complaint management. This is neither neutral nor fair for anyone involved, including HR. Organizations need a complaints process staffed with trained people who understand the challenges of dealing with bullying. That unit requires the authority to create a process that is managed by unbiased, bully-trained investigators who have ample authority to carry out an investigation. This includes the power to interview anyone they deem appropriate and to be provided access to the workplace and people in order to do this difficult job.

Often, the best means to achieve this end is to establish a relationship with a consulting firm that has both the expertise and lack of bias to do this work. Perhaps this isn't common knowledge but there are firms throughout the world to help organizations resolve bullying challenges. These firms specialize in the prevention and management of workplace bullying issues and conflicts. They usually incorporate talented counselors, psychologists, and conflict-resolution experts to ensure they have all the tools necessary to assist. They have no preconceived notions, nothing at risk, and, provided they can do their job free from influence and intervention, this is a superb choice of process.

The difference outside subject matter experts can make is often the difference between a successful intervention/resolution and a HR, financial, and employee-morale disaster. Unbiased, outside experts get to the root of the issues quickly, find opportunities for effective intervention, and address the complex interpersonal challenges. Most importantly, they often resolve difficult problems so that everyone feels satisfied and relationships are preserved. Bringing focus and professional expertise to a bully-engaged workplace, I have seen units move from stressed to blessed with the help of a gifted workplace bullying expert. The return on investment that results is profound. Instead of lawsuits, severance, staff turnover, and high drama, there is compromise, change, rehabilitation, and improved team engagement.

Finally, the investigators should have recommendation-making authority and there must be proper conflict-resolution processes available to effectively manage the next steps. Using standard models for dealing with normal conflicts doesn't work with bullying. This is supported by workplace bullying consulting firms. Unless the conflict-resolution process is sensitive to the power dynamic at play and the nature of victim/offender relationships, most interventions won't succeed.

Experts use a specially constructed form of mediation that incorporates the relationship dynamic and prevents the dysfunction from poisoning the process. The process must be fair to all and, ideally, the investigators and conflict-resolution facilitators must be able to make binding decisions. Once the power play is stifled, the process can focus on collaborative resolution. It is amazing to watch the "impossible" take place with the help of a talented facilitator. Fear, hate, and revenge can move to compromise, understanding, compassion, and healing.

Lack of Trained HR/Staff

Despite their best efforts, many HR personnel are unprepared or lack the authority to address bullies. They also face a difficult choice – they have the organization's best interests as their priority but they see what is really going on. Often, they don't have the training or capacity to take action against the bully. Regardless of their best intention and desire to help, the most common result is that they fail the organization and contribute to the problem.

This plays out to the benefit of the bully and the detriment of the target. Most of the time, the moment a target raises the bullying flag to HR, they respond with fear and think about the organization's protection. Usually that means that they view the complaint as a threat to the company, a liability, a lawsuit waiting to happen, and a PR nightmare in the shadows. As professionals working for the company, they go into risk-management mode, often seeking advice from legal, and likely developing an exit strategy for the target. In effect, they focus all their effort on managing the target and protecting the bully.

Most organizations haven't grasped that HR staff aren't prepared or trained to deal with bullies. None of the standard conflict-management strategies are effective because bullies can't be reasoned with. People tend to believe that they can persuade, apply logic, or collaboratively resolve bullying conflicts. This ignores the general nature of bullies and the genesis of their motivation.

***

The above are the main reasons why organizations fail to respond effectively to bullying situations. There are undoubtedly others that I have failed to mention. What is important is that even though the vast majority of leaders acknowledge bullying is a very serious problem and should be eradicated, very few actually do.

There's a Bully in Our Midst – Now What?

What happens when organizations are forced to respond to a bullying situation? According to the Workplace Bullying Institute the breakdown of employer responses to reports of workplace bullying is distressing. It paints a disturbing picture that rewards the bully and punishes the victim about 70% of the time.[5]

Employers find a way to deny, rationalize, or discount the severity or even the existence of the problem. "It will resolve itself over time." "Once this very challenging project is over, things will calm down." "We can't afford to deal with this right now but we will after our year-end." "We plan on talking to him in his performance review about his leadership style."

Those are just a sampling of the reasons for inaction. Many organizations also take the position that bullying is really a case of two people who just don't work well together or can't get along. They think the individuals can or should work it out. They may even try to organize a meeting with everyone to "hash things out."

> **He that is good for making excuses is seldom good for anything else.**
>
> *Benjamin Franklin*[6]

Even more sobering is the fact that many bullies are defended and even encouraged. We've already noted how focusing on results can easily blind executives to how those results are obtained and the poison that is infiltrating the workplace psyche.

The most common resolution of bullying complaints is that the target is punished in one form or another. The target will either leave/quit, be transferred (which is effectively a demotion), be fired, or be forced to quit (perhaps with a severance package). Rare is the organization that takes direct action punishing or terminating the bully. Ironically, in cases where the bully is facing accountability for her actions, it is common for her to quit instead of looking to rehabilitate. This makes perfect sense given the narcissistic tendencies of bullies – emotional intelligence is necessary for humility, remorse, and amends.

If the bully leaves or is forced out, organizations regularly take the position that the problem is solved. In a previous chapter I told a story of a company that fired a vice president bully – well done! However, they promoted the bully's mentor into the position. Bullying isn't like a carpet stain – apply "Bully Be Gone" and it will look just like new. It is a stain that leaves a permanent cultural mark if nothing more is done. Before long, it dawned on the company that they had a copycat bully. Another bully fired – well done! The total cost to the organization would make any CEO cringe.

Often, organizations make no effort to ensure that the workplace culture is re-focused, reassured, and given a chance to recover. It takes time and engagement from management to heal a broken work environment. In one situation, after the bully departed, the unit continued to bleed talent, for months and even years later. There continued to be a sense of fear, a lack of team spirit, and general malaise that permeated the unit. From an outsider's perspective it was so obvious why the losses continued, yet no one on the inside did anything.

It takes little investment to ensure those left behind are given an opportunity to process, discuss, and shed their shattered levels of engagement. Like a death in the family, the emotional elephant in the room only gets bigger and the scars rarely heal without compassion and communication.

Once again, I stress the value of engaging workplace bullying experts to provide support and strategies for healing and helping workplaces recover from a bullying situation. Their impact can be profound – bringing back trust, improving employee engagement and re-establishing positive workplace culture.

> **A man without ethics is a wild beast loosed upon this world.**
>
> *Albert Camus*[7]

***

Employers aren't exactly rushing to stop bullying at work when it occurs. The most common resolution is that the bully is managed while the target is punished.

An Organizational Anti-bullying Action Plan

Now that we know bullying is bad for business and there are many arguments for eliminating bullying. Let's shift the focus to motivating change and inspiring hope. Governments are slowly responding and initiating profound change. If there are anti-bullying laws in effect, every organization should take action to ensure they are in compliance with the law. Even then, mere compliance shouldn't be the goal – instead, a sincere desire to change and create a workplace culture that motivates and inspires everyone should drive the anti-bullying movement.

Regardless of whether governments have yet to take action, it is reassuring that every organization can take action that will have tremendous permanent impact. There are experts to help, training and tools that are readily available, and a lot of online resources to guide the way. It requires investment, committed leadership, and a sincere desire to implement change; however, the investment is small compared to the risk that organizations are eliminating.

Throughout the world, business-savvy organizations are taking increasingly preventative steps to confront workplace bullying, reinforcing their ethical awareness and instilling confidence in employees and those who do business with them. It is far better to proactively and directly address the bullying than to permit spreading poison throughout the organization.

There are a host of proactive and preventative measures

that motivated organizations can take. Some of the most practical, proactive tips are the following:

a) Establish or revise Respectful Workplace Policies

Create organizational anti-bullying policies, effective methods to report and investigate alleged bullying, and make training mandatory. All organizations should establish clear and effective bullying policies and procedures for addressing bullying allegations. If your organization has no anti-bullying policy, employees, managers, and HR staff should lobby hard for change. If your organization needs help creating these policies, there are people like me that you can turn to for guidance.

b) Initiate awareness campaigns

As noted earlier, there remains a lack of awareness regarding workplace bullying. Many people lack the tools and knowledge to identify bullies and understand the situation once a bully has been identified. Thus, it is essential that everyone in the organization be provided with baseline information and a bully-awareness tool kit.

Senior management must lead the awareness campaign, showing authentic engagement. Their level of involvement provides a strong message for staff and managers. I strongly recommend that you consult with a workplace bullying expert to ensure that your materials and campaign strategy are successful. It is essential that the leaders taking charge of these initiatives be able to articulate with clarity and inspiration the value and mission of the campaign.

c) Invest in training

Training, awareness, and education are critical to the success of such policies. Human resources must be on board and not feel unprepared. Each segment of the organization requires training adapted for the audience. Executives and leaders have different responsibilities and points of focus than do employees. Once again, I recommend that organizations invest in a workplace bullying training expert to ensure that your materials and delivery strategy are successful. This training is specialized and requires sensitivity. Working closely with organizations, workplace bullying experts tailor-make a training program aligned with your work culture and coach you through the implementation process.

d) Walk the walk

There is no replacement for authentic, engaged leadership. Just like any important initiative, unless everyone witnesses sincere, meaningful, and consistent anti-bullying messages and behavior from the executives, the goal will never be reached. It may be cliché, but to eliminate bullying the change must come from and be led by example from the top.

From the CEO and senior managers all the way down to lower-ranking staff, the message must be direct, consistent, and clear – there is zero tolerance for bullying. Even the slightest hint that it might be tolerated is often enough for a bully to cause damage. For leaders that need additional support, workplace bullying coaching for executives and managers is often very helpful.

e) Improve performance management strategies

One of the most effective ways to improve organizational workplace culture is to include performance metrics for respectful behavior and attitude in performance plans for every employee. Give managers a tool to directly address bad behavior the moment it surfaces. By making the employees accountable for disrespectfulness, organizations increase the impact of their workplace respect policies.

f) Implement fair reporting processes

Establish fair, effective, and safe methods to report

alleged bullying: Bullying isn't like other conflicts in the workplace. It requires specialized processes and methods for conflict resolution. First, an unbiased, safe, and user-friendly complaint-reporting process is essential. This works to everyone's benefit and will ensure impartial, confidential, and trustworthy processes.

g) Establish investigation processes

Bullying investigations must be impartial, fair, and fulsome: In order for staff to feel safe and have faith that their employer takes this issue seriously, it is essential that investigations are unbiased, confidential, free from political interference, and result in appropriate responses if allegations are proven. An impartial investigator should be engaged to conduct this sensitive work and be permitted to speak to anyone who may have witnessed the activity. Fair treatment for all alleged victims, bullies, and witnesses is needed to engender trust in the process. I've already discussed the value of firms that specialize in the prevention and management of workplace bullying issues and conflicts. They usually incorporate talented counsellors, psychologists, and conflict-resolution experts to ensure they have all the tools necessary to assist. Particularly in the areas of investigation, intervention, and conflict management, these firms are the lights at the end of a drama-filled tunnel.

h) Take all bullying reports seriously

Take bullying claims seriously but tread carefully. Until there has been a thorough assessment of the complaint by unbiased and trained personnel, the organization should remain neutral. The important point here is that organizations should respond immediately and professionally.

While every report of bullying or bullying-type behavior should be taken seriously, whether they have merit is for the investigation process to determine. It is fair to say that some allegations will turn out to be situations that involve conflict between two competitive staff, or misunderstandings, or communication breakdowns. Regardless, the investigation will provide the organization with a neutral report that helps senior management address the problem, whatever it turns out to be.

i) Use effective conflict-resolution strategies

Normal conflict-resolution processes won't work with bullies: It is naïve to think that you can reason with a bully. Holding a meeting with the bully to "hash out" management's concerns will usually result in the bully defending their actions, using deceit, blame, and deflection as their primary means to convince management the problem lies with the target. In other words, there will be no progress, no accountability.

The most common next step is the bully will take out even greater revenge on the target, assuming she/he is responsible for initiating the complaint against the bully. The net result from management's attempt to reason with the bully is that life for the target gets progressively worse.

I'm not suggesting that conflict-resolution strategies don't work with bullies – on the contrary. As already noted, they are successful if the conflict-resolution process is sensitive to the power dynamic at play and the nature of victim/offender relationships. Organizations need the help of experts using an approach that incorporates the bullying relationship dynamic. Once the power play is stifled, the process can focus on collaborative resolution.

A good example to use is mediation. Without special training, normal mediation is often simply another opportunity for the bully to misbehave and instill fear in the target. However, a gifted facilitator with a background in workplace bullying can quickly eliminate the toxic relationship dynamic with tact and sensitivity. The facilitator will seek opportunities to find compromise, establish accountability, and craft a framework for moving forward. What appeared to be a hopeless mess can turn around with a skilled professional and a motivated organization. There is even a chance for bully rehabilitation.

Sometimes the dynamic requires arbitration. When the bullying conflict-resolution expert is provided with impactful decision-making authority, even the most challenging bully is usually tamed. Without any power left to wield, the bully either becomes engaged or runs. Often, the organization will find it doesn't get this far – if a bully isn't sincere about changing, he/she often departs before the arbitration process begins. If, on the other hand, there is authentic desire to improve, bullies can turn their leadership values around.

***

With all of these policies and processes in place, there is no guarantee that your organization won't ever face a bullying situation. However, when it happens, it will be prepared to handle the challenges effectively, with due process. If there is a bully in the midst, there are mechanisms for quickly snuffing out the problem. Bullies beware – change is coming!

7

Anti-bullying Action Plans for the Individual

A Senior Executive Anti-bullying Action Plan

For those in the executive ranks, use your influence and authority to make change. You have many strong arguments to convince those who challenge change. It won't be easy, but your organization has put you in a leadership role for a reason. Leadership may sometimes feel lonely and difficult – do the right thing anyway. As we heard from Desmond Tutu, "neutrality isn't an option."

> You have enemies? Good. That means you've stood up for something, sometime in your life.
>
> *Winston Churchill, Former Prime Minister of the United Kingdom*[1]

Your action plan incorporates leading your organization to implement its own anti-bullying action plan discussed in Chapter 6. It also incorporates the following plan for managers in terms of demonstrating your own commitment to respectful workplace culture. In addition, there are some actions that you can take to leverage your authority and motivate positive change towards a bully-free zone at work.

Get informed

In order to appear credible, it's important to have the knowledge and capacity to speak with authority. As noted earlier, there is an abundance of information about workplace bullying available. There are also experts available with whom you can consult.

> **It is better to lead from behind and to put others in front, especially when you celebrate victory when nice things occur. You take the front line when there is danger. Then people will appreciate your leadership.**
>
> *Nelson Mandela[2]*

Not only must you be fully informed about bullying, but also about the benefits of a bully-free workplace. Further, when planning for change, it's helpful to have a deep awareness of your organizational culture and historical reality. Identify your allies and the change-intolerant. Appreciate the hurdles that you and the organization will need to overcome.

Get a plan

As with all organizational change initiatives, there is no replacement for a well laid-out business plan and strategy. Identify and consult with all stakeholders. Begin conversations with your cheerleaders to plant the seeds for change. Demonstrate proof of the return on investment. Seek the assistance of subject matter experts. Engage with HR. Devise a plan and courageously move it forward.

Engage others with influence

Within every organization there are people in positions with significant political influence and decision-making authority. Like all successful strategies, you will need their support. They may very well become the sponsors of the program. It's equally important to know who the foes are. Develop a strategy for addressing their concerns and for the possibility that they will openly oppose the anti-bullying initiative. The more you appreciate change management strategies, the better prepared you will be when the naysayers try to de-rail your strategy.

Use examples from other organizations

For many executives and senior managers, the motivation for change is derived from a desire to keep up with or gain advantages against the competition. They also are focused on their own reputation and opportunities. By using very persuasive and factual examples from other organizations rather than anecdotal references, you will earn credibility points.

If you can turn the dialogue into a "what's in it for me" discussion, focusing on how an anti-bullying program advances the agendas of both the organization and the executives, buy-in is more likely. Instead of a focus on what it costs to implement change, perhaps it will be more effective to focus on what it will cost if they do nothing. Lost opportunity cost and return on investment is language that executives relate to.

Incorporate change management into your plan

It is naïve to expect that workplace culture change is easy to implement. Critical to all project plans is the incorporation of sound change management practices. The test of success isn't whether your organization has implemented an anti-bullying program – it is whether it is working, embraced, and effective. There are many tactics for ensuring high levels of adoption and for testing levels of acceptance when implementing change. From effective and continuous training to performance metrics that measure success, incorporate change management strategies in the plan.

Be courageous and unwavering

There will be people who will try to roadblock your work. Known bullies in your organization will immediately begin to work against your initiative, using their supporters in the executive ranks. Expect arguments that focus on the program being a waste of time and money, unnecessary (because bullying isn't a problem), or without merit compared to other organizational priorities. Stay steadfast and firm in your commitment. Leadership isn't about popularity – it is about doing what is right and inspiring change.

***

As a senior executive, you have the influence and authority to activate change. It won't be easy or quick, but your change leadership could permanently alter the course of your organization. It will undoubtedly shape your destiny as a leader. Be strategic and use your network of power brokers. Devise a plan and be courageous. A bully-free workplace will serve you and everyone in your organization, paying dividends far beyond your expectations.

An Action Plan for Human Resources Professionals

As your organization's chief "people person," human resource professionals have the potential for significant influence. You regularly advise the executives and have a unique perspective to share with them. You have a deep awareness about what's going on with everyone working throughout the organization. In fact, HR professionals are often the only ones with a complete picture of the workplace culture. As a result, I believe you are a critical pivot point for change and that you wield persuasive power to help eliminate bullying.

> **Nothing is impossible, the word itself says "I'm possible!"**
>
> *Audrey Hepburn*[3]

I appreciate that HR also finds many challenges when attempting to prevent and respond to bullying. As I've noted, many organizations lack awareness of both the nature of workplace bullying and the depth of its impacts. Further, senior executives regularly condone and even support well-known bullies thanks to their talent for achieving short-term results that impress. Some workplace cultures have even entrenched bullying as a leadership style. This means that you will encounter ignorance, disinterest, and even dismissive attitudes when implementing your anti-bullying action plan. You'll need courage, persistence, and a carefully laid out plan.

As a former senior executive who regularly intersected with HR, I empathize that human resources personnel often feel "caught in the middle": You see the bullying problem (and who the bullies are) and what it's costing (sick leave, stress leave, loss of talented staff, conflicts, team de-motivation, reputation loss). You may also feel conflicted in your role – when acting in the best interests of your organization, you may feel that you're forced to do things that support a workplace bully. In effect, you have to choose between the bullies and the "others" who are impacted by the bully.

HR is often mistakenly used as the bullying complaint office and expected to handle complaints, investigations, and conflict resolution. Simply put, HR staff aren't prepared or properly trained to deal with bullies. Further, HR isn't appropriately placed to ensure that complaints processes are fair, unbiased, and free from influence. Finally, many executives fail to appreciate that bullying situations are highly complex and require bullying experts in order for the situations to be effectively resolved. HR lacks training in counseling, psychology, and the power-dynamic-laden conflict-resolution process, all of which are needed to manage bullying situations.

Despite these potential hurdles, if HR can provide solid reasons to implement change and frame their arguments using words and approaches that executives relate to, I believe there are many opportunities for positive change. Employers are slowly becoming more informed of the many negative work culture and organizational costs associated with bullying. By demonstrating many examples of quantifiable impacts that affect organizational success, innovation, employee engagement, and the bottom line, human resources personnel can make a difference.

Given the HR professional's central location, it makes sense that your action plan contains elements of both the broader organizational action plan and those of senior executives. Like executives, your action plan incorporates leading your organization to implement its own anti-bullying action plan discussed in Chapter 6. It also incorporates some of the plan for managers in terms of demonstrating your own commitment to positive change towards a bully-free zone at work. However, your plan focuses on an approach unique to HR and on ensuring the people in the organization are paramount.

Specifically, your action plan focuses on the following:

- To become well informed about bullying;
- To convince executives to invest in anti-bullying training, policies, and processes;
- To improve organizational awareness;
- To develop methods to quantify the costs of bullying in your organization;

- To ensure HR doesn't become the bullying complaint in-take and resolution office; and
- To take action within your sphere of control and influence to prevent, effectively manage, and eliminate bullying.

Get informed

In order to appear credible when approaching your stakeholders, it's important to have the knowledge and capacity to speak with authority. There is a lot of information about workplace bullying available and experts available with whom you can consult. It's essential that you know about the benefits of a bully-free workplace – in particular, the cost-savings of taking action to prevent and eliminate bullying. As an HR professional, you already have a deep awareness of your organizational culture and historical reality. I have no doubt that you know the bullies and the problems they are creating. To persuade decision-makers to change, you'll need to identify your allies and the change-intolerant. Appreciate the hurdles that you and the organization will need to overcome.

Get a plan

As with all complex projects (and this is a real project), you need to draft a well laid-out business plan and strategy. Identify and consult with all stakeholders. Begin conversations with your cheerleaders to plant the seeds for change. Demonstrate proof of the costs of the bully and quantify them wherever possible. Seek the assistance of subject matter experts. Devise a plan and move it forward.

Be courageous and expect resistance

This project will encounter some unpleasant and difficult people – stand firm. You are doing your job to create the best workplace environment and support everyone in your organization. Known bullies will immediately begin to work against you, using their supporters in the executive ranks. Expect arguments. Stay steadfast in your commitment.

Focus on costs and impacts

As HR, you have information that no one else does – what the bully is costing (sick leave, stress leave, loss of talented staff, conflicts, team de-motivation, reputation loss). This is your most important tool for gaining the attention of the executives. Stay away from the personal when making a pitch for action. Instead, prove that the bully is costing the organization money and show how. Further, prove that the cost of inaction is far greater than the cost of prevention or addressing an active bullying problem.

For example, you have data on how many sick leave days were taken in the bully's unit. You know how many talented employees left their roles. You know how much it cost to replace them (the general rule is replacing an employee costs 1.5 times their salary). You know the costs of severance, investigation experts, and legal advice that were paid. If you can use information from previous bullying events to support your arguments, this will add credibility to your position. Pull all this information together and present it in a concise, factual summary.

If you don't have all the costs, then focus on the impacts. Use as many facts as you can and avoid anecdotal references and stories (unless they are really helpful). When you have someone's ear, focus the conversation on how the bully's behavior is hurting the workplace. Talk about how it's affecting morale and performance. Speak the language that executives relate to – motivate them by putting yourself in their shoes and finding an undeniable "what's in it for me" proposition.

Finally, make sure you present the executive with practical, implementable solutions. Carefully consider what is realistic given your workplace culture. Offer a range of options and make a recommendation. In other words, draft a business plan for going forward. This is a document that executives are comfortable with and will appreciate. Make it as easy and clear as you can. Show them the return on investment of implementing your recommendations. Ask yourself – "What does the executive need to hear from me?" That will guide you to crafting powerful persuasive arguments they will be motivated to act upon. Prove that taking preventative steps to confront workplace bullying is far better than permitting spreading poison throughout the organization.

Work on establishing effective anti-bullying policies, procedures, and best practices

In the background, you can influence positive change towards your organization's overall anti-bullying program. Bring your HR perspective, skills, and influence to the table to convince your organization that it needs to take action. There are a host of proactive and preventative measures HR personnel can take (or at least influence and support). These are referenced in other action plans and include the following:

- Be inspirational leaders – courageously lobby for change.
- Establish or revise Respectful Workplace Policies to specifically include bullying.
- Initiate workplace bullying awareness campaigns.
- Invest in training adapted to each audience (i.e. executives, managers, and staff).
- Improve performance management strategies that include behavioral components that enhance workplace culture.
- Address bad behavior immediately and set a strong leadership example. Avoid having HR become the bullying complaint office.
- Establish investigation processes that are impartial, fair, and fulsome.

- Take bullying claims seriously but tread carefully – until there has been a thorough assessment of the complaint by unbiased and trained personnel, the organization should remain neutral.

- Use conflict-resolution processes that are sensitive to the power dynamic at play and the nature of victim/offender relationships.

- Seek the advice of workplace bullying experts – treat bullying as you would treat any other complex problem that requires specialized professionals to advise and assist. The investment is small compared to the risk your organization is eliminating.

***

There are many things HR personnel can do to confront bullying, motivate change, and help implement an anti-bullying strategy. As trusted advisors to the senior executives, you are a critical pivot point for change. You wield persuasive power to help eliminate bullying. Use it.

A Manager/Unit Leader Action Plan

There are many things managers can do to confront bullying, even if your organization has yet to implement an anti-bullying strategy. It begins with you and your leadership style. By setting your personal code of conduct and ensuring that everyone you lead with aligns their performance and behavior, you can have significant positive impact.

It can take constant vigilance to keep the workplace respectful and free from bullying. Managers can use several strategies to keep their own behavior in check and to foster civility among others. They include the following:

Keep yourself in check

Managers set the tone and create the standards for behavior. Be aware of your actions and consider how you come across to your team and in your workplace. If you eye-roll when you are frustrated or lose your patience, you effectively communicate to your team that they are free to act the same. Disrespect and prepare to be disrespected back.

Be a behavioral role model

In a survey, the Workplace Bullying Institute found that:

> *25% of managers who admitted to having behaved badly said they were uncivil because their leaders—their own role models—were rude. If employees see that those who have climbed the corporate ladder tolerate or embrace bullying behaviour, they're likely to follow suit. So turn off your iPhone during meetings, pay attention to questions, and follow up on promise.*[4]

Solicit others' feedback

It is healthy and an empowering leadership tool to seek reality checks from the people who work with or for you. Such feedback can prove very insightful and helpful. It also shows you are interested in learning and improving. You can't expect your team to learn from you if you aren't willing to do the same.

As a manager, it is important to create an environment where staff are encouraged to speak up. At a minimum, seek regular feedback in safe and confidential ways from your team. Ensure any survey or 360-degree review process includes questions about your leadership style, the level of respect and value that staff feel, and what you could do to improve.

Teach respect

It's amazing how many managers don't understand what it means to be respectful. In one *Harvard Business Review* survey it was found that "one quarter of ill-mannered managers surveyed said that they didn't recognize their behavior as disrespectful."[5] This sounds hard to believe yet it is true. It isn't helpful to condone rudeness by arguing that society has lost all awareness of basic manners and politeness. Do you want to be a leader or a follower? Do what you can to teach respect.

Create rules for group engagement

Even without a workplace respect policy, as a manager, establishing team rules for behavior can have an impact on your team. It can also enhance their performance, team engagement, and job satisfaction. Why not begin a conversation with your team about the kinds of behavior they expect from each other? By getting your staff involved, they are more likely to embrace whatever ground rules for respect they have helped create. It can be as simple as agreeing that no one interrupts when another is speaking, arriving on time, and shutting off devices during meetings. It seems trite or obvious yet so many managers miss this opportunity.

Performance manage

Performance management is an important component for a respectful work environment. As so aptly noted by Christine Porath and Christine Pearson in a 2013 article in the *Harvard Business Review*:

> *Collegiality should be a consideration in every performance review, but many companies think only about outcomes and tend to overlook damaging behaviors. What behavior does your review system motivate? All too often we see organizations badly miss the mark. They want collaboration, but you'd never know it from their evaluation forms, which focus entirely on individual assessment, without a single measure of teamwork, attitude, or respectfulness.[6]*

If you can, revise the performance metrics to include

behavioral components that enhance workplace culture. This creates a culture of accountability and positive reinforcement. If you don't have that authority, lobby for change. In the meantime, it takes little effort to recognize and thank people who behave well, even if your organization isn't ready to put behavioral metrics in the performance strategy.

On the flip side, it is equally important to address bad behavior from the moment it starts. Drawing lines in the sand is essential, even if it feels confrontational or uncomfortable. How can you expect people to improve if you're not ready to have that hard conversation with them about their disrespectful behavior? As a manager, it is your responsibility to lead. That includes courageously addressing bad behavior quickly and assertively.

Organizations often avoid taking action, though, and most incidents go unreported, partly because employees know nothing will come of a report. Set your own course and show that you expect more from your team. If you want to foster respect, take complaints seriously and follow up.

***

A warning to those who think consistent workplace respect is an extravagance: Just one habitually offensive employee critically positioned in your organization can cost you dearly in sick leave costs, lost employees, diminished performance, lost customers, and lost productivity. It can also cost you your job and reputation as an effective manager.

An Action Plan for Targets

If you are a target of a workplace bully, it's reassuring to know that there are many things you can do to protect yourself and create a plan for coping. Having a plan provides much comfort, alleviating the sense of helplessness, solitude, and fear that targets face. It gives you a sense of focus and purpose aside from simply surviving another day at work.

The target action plan contains two separate sections. The first is a discussion of what positive actions targets can take. The second contains overarching considerations that help targets ensure they maintain perspective.

> **A hero is an ordinary individual who finds the strength to persevere and endure in spite of overwhelming obstacles.**
>
> *Christopher Reeve*[7]

Targets can use several strategies to both cope and address the bully at work. They include the following:

Stay healthy

There are many health risks associated with bullying. Constantly check in with yourself to ensure your health is stable. Without your health, nothing else matters. The risk is real.

Develop strategies for ensuring you are taking care of yourself (i.e. regular doctor visits, heart-to-heart conversations with trusted advisors and family, exercise/stress-reduction programs). It is very easy to lose sight of the health impacts that bullying is inflicting upon you. You may need to take sick leave or vacation time to protect your health, or take breaks. Make them a part of your plan. Don't waiver or feel this represents weakness. In fact, it represents you taking back power.

Educate yourself

It is essential to understand what bullying is and how it is carried out in order to move forward. Step 1 in the education process is to get informed. Knowledge is indeed power. Often targets lack a deep awareness of the impact and genesis of bullying. Do some research to ensure you understand what is behind bullying, why you have been targeted, what you've been through, what your feelings are, etc. This will not only demystify the bullying experience, it will help align your expectations, goals, and action plan with reality.

Step 2 of the education process is doing your investigative homework. Find out all of the pieces of the bullying puzzle before you even try to figure out what to do. Some of the most important pieces of the puzzle include the following:

- Whether there are policies in place related to workplace behavior (and what they contain);
- What training, if any, has been provided or is available relating to workplace respect;
- Whether there is legislation that might impact the situation (i.e. anti-bullying, human rights);
- Whether there is a formalized complaints process for employees and, if so, whether it is fair, safe, and effective;
- Whether others have complained and, if so, what was the result;
- What is the general workplace culture and the history of how issues related to disrespectful behavior have been handled;
- Whether HR is well-trained or have handled a bullying scenario before;
- How long the bully has been employed and what influence she/he has;
- The engagement level of senior management and whether they actually care or are aware enough to respond;
- Whether you have any close allies (coworkers or influencers) willing and unafraid to assist; and
- Any other relevant aspect of your workplace bully and culture that you think is important.

Document everything you learn (but not on your work computer). The more detailed and the more objective, the better. This process will both focus you away from feeling victimized and ensure that whatever strategy you create, it aligns with your workplace reality and appropriately sets your expectations.

Do a self-check

With all the information in hand, do a self-check and consider whether you might be misinterpreting the behavior, overreacting to it, or whether you've unknowingly contributed to the problem. I know from experience that some of my engagement contributed to the bullying problem. By losing our patience, acting out, fighting back at the wrong time, baiting the bully, or other unchecked responses, we may not be doing ourselves any favors.

Do your best work

While you complete your investigation and devise your plan, do your best work. Try to maintain your integrity and professionalism. Easy to say but hard to do when you're in such a toxic and difficult situation. Try not to sabotage yourself or the bully and don't create additional performance issues for the bully to jump on. Sometimes there may be ways for you to devise some tactics in order to avoid, placate, or ignore the bully. For example, it may help to stroke the aggressor's ego. Even a small gesture, such as ending an email with "Thanks so much for your help" or complimenting the person on something, can help. Without being sycophantic, give it a try and see if it has an impact.

Don't blame yourself

It is almost a given that you will assume the problem and situation is your fault when it's not. The bully chose you based on her/his warped perception of the world and what is a threat. It's normal to think that you must be doing something wrong for someone to treat you this way at work. Given the fact that you are likely one of the most competent and diligent employees, it's equally understandable that your response is to try to fix the situation by working harder and proving your worth.

Remember to step back and appreciate that the bully is acting aggressively because he/she feels threatened by you.

This has little to do with the work, or you, and everything to do with the bully's messed-up mind.

Stand up for yourself

I appreciate that much of what you can do depends on the workplace and local culture. Nonetheless, bullies are known to step back if the target defends himself. Don't be afraid to call out the bad behavior when it happens. I believe very strongly in making immediate corrections. If the bully says something inappropriate (i.e. calling you "stupid" or condescending like "honey" in a meeting), respond right then: "I don't like being called that. Please use my name."

If you're uncomfortable with an immediate, public response, say something as soon as you're able. After the meeting, you could say, "I didn't like being called 'Honey.' It demeans me." Show that there is no reward for treating you that way. The message should be: "Don't mess with me; it won't be worth your effort."

This line drawing is useful because it may lead to an opportunity to try to solve it informally. Bullies aren't fools (far from it) – they might reassess the situation and back away. This is especially possible if you take serious note that you have a bully in your midst and assess what you might be able to do to reduce the bully's perception that you are threatening. Act accordingly and it may result in a détente of sorts.

Establish a support network

Regardless of your plan, it is important to have sounding boards that are reliable and supportive. In the beginning, it is recommended that these people be outside of your work. Gossiping or sharing your frustrations with a work colleague is likely unhelpful.

Instead, there are trusted mentors, friends, and wise people to turn to. It is important to have a place to vent, to seek feedback, to strategize, and to simply have a shoulder to lean on. Building a support network that can help get you through the tough times makes a significant difference. Also, as hard as it may be, share your feelings openly and without sugarcoating. Those who want to help you can only do their best work if you are honest about the depth and breadth of the problem.

Get counseling (if possible)

Many organizations have Employee Assistance Programs that are confidential – use them. The guidance of trained professionals is a tremendous help to coping and making sure you stay balanced. Being proud won't serve you. You don't have all the tools but others do.

Get a plan

This is the most important step in your strategy. There is simply no replacement for good planning and a clear breakdown of what you need to do. Treat this like a project and create a business plan with all the essential elements. Often the planning process provides a much-needed sense of purpose and focuses work life away from the bully.

Define your goals. This could mean that you're going to create and implement an exit strategy. It could mean you want to gather all the information needed to launch a formal complaint. Regardless, it's important to know what your plan is focused on achieving and what you need to do to get the desired result.

Once you have your goals in place, you'll need to gather information. Outline each task, with a plan for how to obtain the data and a realistic time frame within which to get it. Similar to project management, you also have to determine your scope. How far do you need to go to ensure you have everything, and what are the limits of the plan?

Risk manage as best you can and always try to stay nimble. The bully will continue to operate while you are implementing your plan. Consequently, be ready to adjust and even scrap your plan if necessary.

Also, it is important to identify the stakeholders and assess their impact on your plan. Whether it is HR, your co-workers, other managers, an influential executive, or the bully, each person plays a role in the plan. Thus, your plan should consider how to manage each stakeholder and how he or she helps your plan succeed.

Like any strategy, there are some elements that help drive the likelihood of success. They include the following:

i) Develop an exit strategy.

Regardless of what you hope to achieve, make certain you are also working on an exit strategy. It is possible that the best strategy is to develop your organizational exit plan. It may get so bad that you have to pull the trigger on leaving the job. It's helpful to consider many options for exiting. There are more than you might think.

Some of the obvious exit strategies include quitting, finding a new job (within or outside your current organization), or transferring to another department. There are others, though, such as taking an educational leave, taking sick/ stress leave (this requires doctor support), or hiring a lawyer to intervene on your behalf (i.e. to negotiate a severance package or even launch legal action).

One factor worth mentioning is that targets are prone to let their ego get in the way of healthy and self-preserving decision-making. The Workplace Bullying Institute has done online surveys that show more targets stay in a bullying situation because of pride (40%

of respondents) than because of economics (38%).[8] Rather than worrying about letting the bully win, you're better off focusing on your own well-being.

Regardless of what it contains, an exit strategy is essential to protect yourself if things become impossible or your health is being impacted. You may not be able to change this toxic workplace but you can leave a message about why you left and move onto a harmonious workplace. Insist on an exit interview and even then, write a letter to your CEO telling her/him why you left the organization using as much objective information as possible.

The bottom line is that even if you want to take action against the bully, don't suffer unnecessarily. If the situation persists and you can leave, do it. Try to plan ahead and if you can find a new job while you're still in the toxic one, even better.

ii) Document. Investigate. Secure objective proof.

Aligning these tasks with your action plan goals, the documentation and investigation process is a critical component for success. If your plan is to launch a formal bullying complaint, consider what information would be needed to create the most impactful and effective strategy to present a complaint. How would you obtain this evidence?

Document every incidence of unacceptable behavior but focus on facts you can prove and secure the irrefutable evidence to do it. If there were others who witnessed an event write that down, along with the date, time, place, and explanation of the situation. This is a stealthy challenge and you'll need to be patient, careful, and smart. Just like solving a major crime, you're pulling all the pieces of evidence together to present the most persuasive case possible. Don't put anything on your work computer. Ever.

iii) Know the limitations.

Even if you are clearly being bullied, the chances of change or success in many organizations are low. There is hope with new laws and improved awareness but accept reality. Appreciate the organizational landscape and align your expectations accordingly. Despite even the best arguments or an airtight case, it's sometimes hard for organizations to take action. If you're in an abusive situation at work, the most tenable solution may be to leave — if that's a possibility.

iv) Control what you can.

The only aspect of bullying that you can control is how you respond. As hard as that is to accept, the sooner you can come to terms with your very limited sphere of influence, the more likely your action plan will be realistic.

Don't expect you can control others; particularly those you are hoping are your allies. Even if your coworkers feel terrible about what they are witnessing, they are afraid too. They don't want to become the target. They may not have your back.

Also, before you approach anyone from within, assess the risks and the likely response options. My advice to targets is to appreciate the reality and role of HR: They have the organization's interests paramount. They are assessing the extent of the company's liability. This is especially true if the bully is a member of management. HR is rarely an ally and often makes the situation worse.

Expect realistic reactions from HR, your supervisor, and senior management. Your investigation will provide you with baseline information to help gauge what to expect.

Be courageous but calculated.

Be strategic, focused, and patient. Only move ahead when you are ready. Where you can, call out the inappropriate behavior in the moment. Be prepared for conflict and challenges. Realistically assess the risks and challenges you would face if you raised the flag. Be courageous but sensible.

> You gain strength, courage, and confidence by every experience in which you really stop to look fear in the face. You are able to say to yourself, "I lived through this horror. I can take the next thing that comes along."
>
> *Eleanor Roosevelt*[9]

v) Enlist help, but choose very carefully.

Consider whether you have any colleagues willing to join forces with you – there is power and credibility in numbers. Given that targets are commonly the most respected and well-liked employees, it is likely that you have alliances at work — peers and people above and below, who can be your advocates and champions. When you're ready, talk to those supporters and see what they can do to help, whether it's simply confirming your perspective or speaking on your behalf.

vi) Focus on costs and impacts.

If your plan is to present a complaint, it helps to stay as far away from the personal as possible when making a pitch for action. Even though you have been deeply hurt and personally impacted, don't tell a story of emotional wounds. Make an argument that the bully is costing the organization money and show how. Demonstrate as objectively as possible that harboring the bully is impacting organizational success.

You may want to point to some well-known examples to compare (i.e. recent bad press for Amazon's "Darwinian culture"). When you have someone's ear, focus the conversation on how the bully's behavior is hurting the workplace.

Talk about how it's affecting morale and performance. If people have left, are on sick leave, or projects are failing, these facts are very helpful. Personal pleas rarely work and too often degenerate into "he said-she said" type arguments.

**

A focused, practical, and realistic plan is fundamental to coping with a workplace bully. The goal of the plan may vary but the requirement for a plan is universal. The best way to cope with a workplace terrorist is through a clear strategy that considers all the options and prioritizes the means to achieve the goals of the plan. Taking control of what you can and empowering yourself to deal effectively with the bully will help you avoid making many mistakes and losing sight of your vision.

An Action Plan for Coworkers, Witnesses, and Bystanders

If you are a coworker of a target or a witness from another unit, it's helpful to remember that there are many things you can do to help the target, protect yourself, and create your own plan for coping. To think that coworkers aren't deeply impacted by the bullying is naïve and counter-intuitive. Coworkers suffer many of the target's feelings of anxiety, fear, and stress – work becomes a place of daily struggle, vulnerability, and pain.

Educate yourself about bullying and how those around the organization might respond. Devising your own plan provides much comfort, and alleviates the sense of helplessness, guilt, and fear that witnesses face. It gives you a sense of focus and purpose aside from simply surviving another day at work.

An important point for coworkers is that your plan should consider many of the same factors that form part of the coping strategies for targets. Consequently, your plan must reflect the reality of your workplace, what you can control, what you can do to protect yourself, and how you might be able to assist the target. Every action plan requires a tailor-made strategy.

There are many similarities between a target's action plan and that of a witness but viewed through a different lens. The best advice for coping for coworkers is to create an action plan that incorporates the following:

Stay healthy

There are many health risks associated with bullying suffered by coworkers and bystanders. Watching a friend or colleague being broken down by a campaign of interpersonal destruction is no different than witnessing a violent crime. There are emotional and physical reactions that are natural and can negatively affect you. Constantly check in with yourself to ensure your health is stable.

Develop strategies for ensuring you are taking care of yourself (i.e. regular doctor visits, heart-to-heart conversations with trusted advisors and family, exercise/stress-reduction programs).

Educate yourself

Just like for targets, Step 1 in the education process is to get informed. Often witnesses lack a deep awareness of the impact and genesis of bullying. This leads to a sense of utter helplessness because you don't comprehend the chaos.

Do some research so that you understand why your colleague has been targeted, and what you're feeling. This will not only demystify the bullying experience, it will help you understand the mix of emotions you are experiencing. For example, it helps to appreciate that it is normal to feel fear each day at work – fear for what may happen to the target, fear that you may become a target, fear of uncertainty, and other fears. It further comforts when you learn that witnesses commonly feel "witness paralysis," which leads to feelings of guilt because you have done nothing to either help the target or confront the bully. With helpful information you will be better able to align your expectations, goals, and action plan with reality.

Do your best work

In an effort to avoid becoming a target while you complete your investigation and devise your plan, do your best work. Try to maintain your integrity and professionalism. Try not to act out emotionally, alerting the bully to the fact you sense something bad is going on. Don't create any performance issues for the bully to jump on. Do your best to stay away from the bully and modify your behavior where appropriate.

Document everything

Regardless of what you ultimately choose to do, it is essential to document every incidence of unacceptable behavior. Focus on facts and securing irrefutable evidence to support your version of the events.

Not only might your documentation help the target in the event of an investigation or formal complaint, it may also help you feel like you are positively contributing to the effort to eliminate the bully. Pull all the pieces of evidence together to present the most persuasive case possible. Prepare as if you were going to be interviewed by a bullying complaint investigator.

Provide support for others

Knowing that you are neither a counselor nor a trained HR staff member, try to do what you can to provide support both to the target and your coworkers. You're all going through an unpleasant time and it helps to feel you are sharing the burden.

Consider what the target is trying to manage and how

you might provide emotional support or other compassionate assistance. Sometimes just listening is enough. Help the target reason things out and make sound decisions given the realities of your workplace.

If called upon or there is a chance, volunteer to be interviewed in the event of a formal complaint and investigation. This is your chance to actively contribute to eliminating bullying and to use the evidence that you carefully acquired. This might take courage and be very uncomfortable but remember the words of Martin Luther King – "The time is always right to do what is right."

Consider a team response

There is truth about the adage of "strength in numbers." This is especially the case regarding bullying. Organizations really wake up when a team raises the flag in a coordinated and well laid-out strategy. Even a few coworkers banding together can have a significant influence. Like targets, if you are going to consider this approach, it is essential to get a plan and work together to implement it. All of the components of the target's action plan should form part of your plan.

If a team response isn't possible, perhaps some coworkers will at least provide support by signing a letter to the executive. There are different ways to lend a hand without being the spokesperson.

Finally, if you decide that you want to lodge your own formal complaint or make a personal plea to an influential executive, it is even more important to get a plan.

Get a plan

With all of the noted plan components to consider, formulate your goals and strategic approach. Focus on identifying the objective negative impacts that the bully is creating for the team and target. The more that you can emphasize the costs, the more likely you will reach your influential empathetic leader.

***

Coworkers, witnesses, and bystanders can play a change leadership role in helping address bullying in the workplace. There is no doubt that such engagement will be difficult and unpleasant. Try to focus on how it will feel to have taken a risk, helped make a difference, and proven the value of integrity, compassion, and team orientation. Perhaps think of the message that it sends to everyone else in the unit, others in your organization, your children, and your friends. Goodness begins in the mirror.

Conclusion

Our greatest weakness lies in giving up. The most certain way to succeed is always to try just one more time.

— Thomas A. Edison[1]

Every workplace seems to have a bully on staff. Workplace bullying is incredibly prevalent and organizations face challenges in effectively addressing or eliminating it. In addition, the impacts of bullying are severe, costly, and felt throughout the organization and even beyond. It is this fact that I believe will eventually stimulate real change.

The good news is that increased public awareness, recent research, and expanding illegalization of workplace bullying are having positive results. Employers around the world are becoming more informed of the impacts and costs associated with bullying. They are seeing more objective data and examples to learn from. The opportunity cost of failing to take action is beginning to resonate for organizations.

While it may seem like the higher goals of doing what is ethical, moral, or responsible matter less, I think that what matters most is that the world is waking up. If the only way that organizations will respond to bullying is by being fed the business case for eliminating bullying, then we should all provide our organizations with the diet of numbers and statistics that will motivate action.

It is a simple fact that if employers and senior executives

take initiative in addressing bullying early on, much larger financial, ethical, legal, human resource, and project problems will be avoided. Eventually, these initiatives will lead to wider support for zero tolerance for bullying in the workplace regardless of circumstance, societal norm, or jurisdiction.

For all of us impacted by bullying, there is much to learn and to do to become part of the movement forward to change. There are action plans and steps that we can take regardless of where we live, where we work, what role we have, and what workplace culture we face. They will be different depending on many factors, but what is important is that we have information and tools to engage effectively. It is my sincere hope that with this handbook, readers feel less afraid, better informed, and properly empowered to courageously address workplace bullying.

Bibliography

Barnes, Patricia G. *Surviving Bullies, Queen Bees and Psychopaths.* United States: Patricia G. Barnes, 2012; updated July 2013.

Cardemil, Alisha R., Esteban V. Cardemil, and Ellen O'Donnell. "Self-Esteem in Pure Bullies and Bully/Victims: A Longitudinal Analysis." *Journal of Interpersonal Violence* (August 2010, Sage Publications) 25 (8): 1489–1502. doi:10.1177/0886260509354579. PMID 20040706.

Einarsen, Ståle. *Bullying and Emotional Abuse in the Workplace: International Perspectives in Research and Practice.* Taylor & Francis, 2003.

Erickson, Ian. "Bullying in the Workplace: A Problem for Employers," *Guardian Newspaper* (February 1, 2014). http://guardianlv.com/2014/02/bullying-in-workplace-a-problem-for-employers/#jVfFzPGYWtSlXGdq.99.

Habib, Marlene. "Bullies Can Make Workplace Intolerable," *The Globe and Mail* (December 19, 2011. Last updated: September 6, 2012). http://www.theglobeandmail.com/report-on-business/small-business/sb-managing/bullies-can-make-workplace-intolerable/article4201840/.

Kantor, Jodi and David Streitfeld. "Inside Amazon: Wrestling Big Ideas in a Bruising Workplace," *The New York Times* (August 16, 2015). http://www.nytimes.com/2015/08/16/technology/inside-amazon-wrestling-big-ideas-in-a-bruising-workplace.html?_r=0.

Kelsey, Lindsay. "The significance of Amazon's work culture — and how the *Times* article may impact the retail giant," Retaildive.com (August 19, 2015). http://www.retaildive.com/news/the-significance-of-amazons-work-culture-and-how-the-times-article-may-i/404192/.

Kouzes, J., and B. Posner. *The Leadership Challenge*. San Francisco, CA: Jossey-Bass, 2008.

Pfeffer, Jeffrey. "3 lessons from the Amazon takedown," Fortune.com (August 18, 2015). http://fortune.com/2015/08/18/amazon-new-york-times/.

Pinsky, Erica. *Road to Respect: Path to Profit*. Canada: 2009.

Porath, Chrisine and Christine Pearson. "The Price of Incivility," *Harvard Business Review* (January 1, 2013). http://hbr.org/2013/01/the-price-of-bullying/ar/1.

Project Management Institute. "PMI Code of Ethics and Professional Conduct" (2006). Accessed August 10 2014. http://www.pmi.org/About-Us/Ethics/Ethics-Resources.aspx.

Project Management Institute. "PMI Ethical Decision-Making Framework" (2013). Accessed July 24 2014. http://www.pmi.org/About-Us/Ethics/Ethics-Resources.aspx.

Stephens, Tina and Jane Hallas. *Bullying and Sexual Harassment: A Practical Handbook*. Elsevier, 2006. p. 94.

The Workplace Bullying Institute website. Accessed July 24 2014. http://www.workplacebullying.org.

Williams, Ray. "How Workplace Bullying Harms every Employee in the Toxic Work Environment," *The Financial Post* (February 21, 2015). http://business.financialpost.com/executive/management-hr/how-workplace-bullying-harms-every-employee-in-the-toxic-environment.

Endnotes

Introduction

1. Michael M. Honda, BrainyQuote.com (retrieved October 27, 2015, from BrainyQuote.com website: http://www.brainyquote.com/quotes/quotes/m/michaelmh519241.html).

2. Clive Boddy, "Bullying and Corporate Psychopaths at Work" (December 3, 2012, available from https://www.youtube.com/watch?v=tlB1pFwGhA4&index=19&list=PLlszBLRhOFq8MTEunsB1psfl_c4EUyyTk).

Chapter 1

1. Martin Luther King, Jr., BrainyQuote.com (retrieved October 27, 2015, from BrainyQuote.com website: http://www.brainyquote.com/quotes/quotes/m/martinluth106169.html).

2. Patricia G. Barnes, *Surviving Bullies, Queen Bees and Psychopaths* (United States: Patricia G. Barnes, 2012; updated July 2013).

3. Jim Kouzes & Barry Posner, *The Leadership Challenge* (San Francisco, CA: Jossey-Bass, 2008).

4. Workplace bullying, 2015, Merriam-webster.com (accessed October 15, 2015, from http://www.merriam-webster.com/dictionary/workplacebullying).

5. Kofi Annan, BrainyQuote.com (retrieved October 27, 2015, from BrainyQuote.com website: http://www.brainyquote.com/quotes/quotes/k/kofiannan389917.html).

6. Ståle Einarsen, *Bullying and Emotional Abuse in the Workplace: International Perspectives in Research and Practice* (Taylor & Francis: 2003).

7. "The WBI Definition of 'Workplace Bullying'" (accessed July 24, 2015; available from http://www.workplacebullying.org/individuals/problem/definition/).

8. "The Definition of Workplace Violence" (accessed October 10, 2015; available from https://www.osha.gov/SLTC/workplaceviolence/).

9. *The Devil Wears Prada* (accessed on October 25, 2015; available from https://en.wikipedia.org/wiki/The_Devil_Wears_Prada_(film)).

10. Antoine de Saint-Exupery, BrainyQuote.com (retrieved October 27, 2015, from BrainyQuote.com website: http://www.brainyquote.com/quotes/quotes/a/antoines137412.html).

11. Margaret Heffernan, BrainyQuote.com (retrieved October 27, 2015, from BrainyQuote.com website: http://www.brainyquote.com/quotes/quotes/m/margarethe556959.html).

12. "PMI Ethical Decision-Making Framework," pmi.org (2013, accessed on July 24 2015; available from http://www.pmi.org/About-Us/Ethics/Ethics-Resources.aspx).

13. Tom Felton, BrainyQuote.com (retrieved October 27, 2015, from BrainyQuote.com website: http://www.brainyquote.com/quotes/quotes/t/tomfelton472945.html).

14. Erica Pinsky, *Road to Respect: Path to Profit* (Canada: 2009), 78.

15. Ray Williams, "How Workplace Bullying Harms every Employee in the Toxic Work Environment" (*The Financial Post*, February 21, 2015. Available from http://business.financialpost.com/executive/management-hr/how-workplace-bullying-harms-every-employee-in-the-toxic-environment).

16. Macklemore, BrainyQuote.com (retrieved October 27, 2015, from BrainyQuote.com website: http://www.brainyquote.com/quotes/quotes/m/macklemore483477.html).

17. Christine Porath and Christine Pearson, "The Price of Bullying in the Workplace" (*Harvard Business Review*, January 1, 2013; available from http://hbr.org/2013/01/the-price-of-bullying/ar/1).

18. Workplace Bullying Institute, workplacebullying.org (available from http://www.workplacebullying.org/wbiresearch/wbi-2014-us-survey/).

19. Jennifer Grasz, "Careerbuilder.com Study Finds More Workers Feeling Bullied in the Workplace," Careerbuilder.com (August 29, 2012; available from http://www.computerweekly.com/news/2240085434/IT-workers-being-bullied-says-union).

20. Clare Rayner, "The Incidence of Workplace Bullying" (*Journal of Community and Applied Social Psychology*, 1997, Vol. 7 No. 3), pp. 199-208.

21. Ståle Einarsen, "The Nature and Causes of Bullying at Work," International Journal of Manpower (*MCB University Press*, 0143-7720: 1999, Vol. 20 No1/2), pp16-27.

22. Rebecca Thomson, "IT Workers Being Bullied, Says Union," Computerweekly.com (March 4, 2008, available from http://www.computerweekly.com/news/2240085434/IT-workers-being-bullied-says-union).

Chapter 2

1. Clarence Thomas, BrainyQuote.com (retrieved October 27, 2015, from BrainyQuote.com website: http://www.brainyquote.com/quotes/quotes/c/clarenceth137493.html).

2. "Treasury Board of Canada Policy on Harassment Prevention and Resolution" (accessed on September 20, 2015; available from http://www.tbs-sct.gc.ca/pol/doc-eng.aspx?id=26041&section=text).

3. Stephanie Pappas, "Work Bully Victims Struggle with Dangerous Stress," Livescience.com (January 12, 2012; available from http://www.livescience.com/17872-workplace-bullying-stress.html).

4. Sam Walton, BrainyQuote.com (retrieved October 27, 2015, from BrainyQuote.com website: http://www.brainyquote.com/quotes/quotes/s/samwalton163394.html).

5. Albert Schweitzer, BrainyQuote.com (retrieved October 27, 2015, from BrainyQuote.com website: http://www.brainyquote.com/quotes/quotes/a/albertschw133530.html).

6. Workplace Bullying Institute, www.workplacebullying. org (available from http://www.workplacebullying.org/ wbiresearch/wbistudies/).

7. Ibid.

8. Octavia E. Butler, BrainyQuote.com (retrieved October 27, 2015, from BrainyQuote.com website: http://www. brainyquote.com/quotes/quotes/o/octaviaeb646144. html).

Chapter 3

1. Jack Welch, BrainyQuote.com (retrieved October 27, 2015, from BrainyQuote.com website: http://www.brainy-quote.com/quotes/quotes/j/jackwelch173308.html).

2. Bono, BrainyQuote.com (retrieved October 27, 2015, from BrainyQuote.com website: http://www.brainyquote. com/quotes/quotes/b/bono129880.html).

Chapter 4

1. Dalai Lama, BrainyQuote.com (retrieved October 27, 2015, from BrainyQuote.com website: http://www.brainy-quote.com/quotes/quotes/d/dalailama386167.html).

2. Pinsky, *Road to Respect*, 63 - 68.

3. Pinsky, *Road to Respect*, 66.

4. Rollo May, BrainyQuote.com (retrieved October 27, 2015, from BrainyQuote.com website: http://www.brainy-quote.com/quotes/quotes/r/rollomay158695.htm).

Chapter 5

1. Herbert Spencer, BrainyQuote.com (retrieved October 27, 2015, from BrainyQuote.com website: http://www. brainyquote.com/quotes/quotes/h/herbertspe109568. html).

2. Pappas, Livescience.com.

3. Workplace Bullying Institute, worplacebullying. org (available from http://www.workplacebullying. org/2012-d/).

4. Workplace Bullying Institute, worplacebullying.org (available from http://www.workplacebullying.org/wbire-search/wbistudies/).

5. Ian Erickson, "Bullying in the Workplace A Problem for Employers" (*Guardian Newspaper*, February 1, 2014).

6. Jodi Kantor and David Streitfield, "Inside Amazon: Wrestling Big Ideas in a Bruising Workplace" (*New York Times*, August 16, 2015).

7. Erickson, *Guardian Newspaper*, February 1, 2014.

Chapter 6

1. Desmond Tutu, BrainyQuote.com (retrieved October 27, 2015, from BrainyQuote.com website: http://www.brainy-quote.com/quotes/quotes/d/desmondtut106145.html).

2. Peter Drucker, BrainyQuote.com (retrieved November 2, 2015, from BrainyQuote.com website: http://www.brainy-quote.com/quotes/quotes/p/peterdruck131069.html).

3. Workplace Bullying Institute, worplacebullying.org (available from http://www.workplacebullying.org/wbi-z-bl-1/).

4. Orrin Woodward, Goodreads.com (retrieved September 18, 2015 from Goodreads.com website: https://www.goodreads.com/author/quotes/249881.Orrin_Wood-ward?page=2).

5. Workplace Bullying Institute, worplacebullying.org (available from http://www.workplacebullying.org/wbire-search/wbi-2014-us-survey/).

6. Benjamin Franklin, BrainyQuote.com (retrieved October 27, 2015, from BrainyQuote.com website: http://www.brainyquote.com/quotes/quotes/b/benjaminfr383794.html).

7. Albert Camus, BrainyQuote.com (retrieved October 27, 2015, from BrainyQuote.com website: http://www.brainy-quote.com/quotes/quotes/a/albertcamu118026.html).

Chapter 7

1. Winston Churchill, BrainyQuote.com (retrieved October 27, 2015, from BrainyQuote.com website: http://www.brainyquote.com/quotes/quotes/w/winstonchu135210.html).

2. Nelson Mandela, BrainyQuote.com (retrieved October 27, 2015, from BrainyQuote.com website: http://www.brainyquote.com/quotes/quotes/n/nelsonmand393048.html).

3. Audrey Hepburn, BrainyQuote.com (retrieved January 19, 2016, from BrainyQuote.com website: http://www.brainyquote.com/quotes/quotes/a/audreyhepb413479.html?src=t_inspirational).

4. Workplace Bullying Institute, worplacebullying.org (available from http://www.workplacebullying.org/wbiresearch/wbistudies/).

5. Christine Porath and Christine Pearson, "The Price of Bullying in the Workplace."

6. Porath and Pearson. Ibid.

7. Christopher Reeve, BrainyQuote.com (retrieved October 27, 2015, from BrainyQuote.com website: http://www.brainyquote.com/quotes/quotes/c/christophe141891.html).

8. Workplace Bullying Institute, worplacebullying.org (available at http://www.workplacebullying.org/wbiresearch/wbi-2014-us-survey/).

9. Eleanor Roosevelt, BrainyQuote.com (retrieved October 27, 2015, from BrainyQuote.com website: http://www.brainyquote.com/quotes/quotes/e/eleanorroo121157.html).

Conclusion

1. Thomas A. Edison, BrainyQuote.com (retrieved October 27, 2015, from BrainyQuote.com website: http://www.brainyquote.com/quotes/quotes/t/thomasaed149049.html).

Paul Pelletier is a corporate lawyer, project manager, international public speaker, and business executive with over 25 years' experience in senior roles in government and industry.

During his career, on more than one occasion, Paul realized he was the target of disrespectful workplace behavior and workplace bullying. He suffered in silence until his health forced him to take a different approach. Leveraging his workplace bullying experiences he is now an advocate, consultant, and expert in workplace respect, diversity, and bullying. Helping organizations establish strategic policies, programs, and processes for openly, fairly, and effectively addressing disrespectful workplace behavior is his focus. He is a regular presenter at global conferences and other events. His website is www.paulpelletierconsulting.com.

Follow him on Twitter: @consulting_pp.